TWO REPUBLICS IN CHINA

TWO REPUBLICS IN CHINA

How Imperial China Became the PRC

X. L. WOO

Algora Publishing
New York

Library of Congress Cataloging-in-Publication Data —

Woo, X. L.
Two republics in China: how imperial China became the PRC / X.L. Woo.
pages cm
ISBN 978-1-62894-096-1 (soft cover: alkaline paper) — ISBN 978-1-62894-
097-8 (hard cover: alkaline paper) — ISBN 978-1-62894-098-5 (ebook) 1. China—
Politics and government—20th century. 2. China—History—Republic, 1912-
1949. 3. China—History—1949-1976. 4. Republics—History—20th century.
5. Communism—China—History—20th century. 6. Social change—China—
History—20th century. 7. Social conflict—China—History—20th century. 8.
China—History, Military—20th century. I. Title.
DS775.7.W66 2014
951.05—dc23
2014026843

Printed in the United States

Also by X. L. Woo

Old Shanghai and the Clash of Revolution, Algora 2013
Empress Wu the Great, Tang Dynasty China, Algora 2008
Empress Dowager Cixi: China's Last Dynasty, Algora 2002

TABLE OF CONTENTS

PART ONE

THE FIRST REPUBLIC—THE REPUBLIC OF CHINA

PART ONE

THE FIRST REPUBLIC—

THE REPUBLIC OF CHINA

CHAPTER 1. 1911: HOW THE LAST DYNASTY CRUMBLED AND WARLORDS TOOK OVER

Rebellion in Wuchang City

A long line of imperial dynasties had held sway over all (or parts) of China from 2100 BCE to 1911. China was a world unto itself for much of these 4,000 years, but history went off its tracks when the British came in. Smoking opium had been a serious crime in China, but for the British opium was big business. And they made it far bigger by slaughtering and pillaging, overwhelming the Chinese by 1842 and forcing them to open up their nation to foreign trade. Soon, British merchants flooded the market with opium grown in India, and millions, perhaps more than 10 million, Chinese were hopelessly addicted. China was reeling and the Qing Dynasty was on the ropes.

The Qing Dynasty (1644–1911) had been established by the Manchus, people that had originated in northeastern China (Manchuria). Although some of their ancestors had periodically been in power in ancient times, it was the Han people that were (and are now) the largest ethnic group in China. The Han could not bear the oppression of these Manchus, whose officials, the Mandarins, were increasingly corrupt. As the Qing Dynasty sank into misery, the Han rose up in a series of rebellions hoping to overthrow the rulers and regain the imperial throne. In an era when some of the ambitious young elite were already studying abroad and learning modern ways, the imperial leaders still maintained a traditional army using ancient weaponry including lances and spears. So the overthrow was easy enough—but what next? Read on, and we'll see.

Sun Yat-sen (1866–1925) was a revolutionary vanguard and he organized the Nationalist Party for the purpose of revitalizing the nation. After a few uprisings were brutally put down, the last successful rebellion broke out in Wuchang City of Sichuan Province, westward along the Yangtze River, upstream from Shanghai. In May of 1911, the Qing government had nationalized or appropriated two railways that were private Chinese companies, without giving the owners any compensation, and then sold them to foreigners. Needless to say, the local people wanted to defend their rights. The most violent reactions took place in Sichuan Province. The Qing government did have a New Army too (trained in the use of guns and cannons), and they sent them in. But in this division, many soldiers and even officers were actually members of the revolutionaries. So some leaders of the Nationalist Party planned a rebellion in the army.

A regiment was camped at the north gate of Wuchang City. Around 6 o'clock, on the 10th of October, many rebellious soldiers marched toward the armory in the city with the intention of seizing it. At that time, in the camp a platoon leader was making his rounds to check on the soldiers and he found that many were absent. He also saw the squad leader was lying on his bed, so he yelled at him, "What are you doing? You want to rebel?" (That's a Chinese way of putting down one's subordinates.) The squad leader never had thought much of his platoon leader, so he replied insolently, "You said I'd rebel. Now I'm rebelling." A soldier standing nearby simply shot the platoon leader dead.

Now the battalion leader came in and he was shot dead, too. Seizing this opportunity, the Nationalist Party's point man in the new army, who was the leader of another squad, declared a rebellion and called for his men to take up their arms right then and there.

Soldiers from many different camps came to their aid, the number reaching more than 3,000. They controlled a cannon field and attacked the governor's residence under the command of Wu Zhaoling, an officer in the eighth battalion. They called themselves the Revolutionary Army. The governor escaped to a warship on the river. The Revolutionary Army occupied the city. Revolutionaries in Hanyang and Hankou cities also raised the banner of rebellion. On the 11th of October, the Revolutionary Army took over Hanyang City and on the 12th day, they occupied Hankou City. Three cities in a row.

The Establishment of the Republic of China

Then the Revolutionary Army founded the military government and asked Li Yuanhong (1864–1928) to be the governor, and they declared the new state to be the Republic of China. At the beginning of November, at the proposal of Song Jiaoren (1882–1913) and some others, a constitution was drafted and called "The Temporary Constitution of Republic of China." It had seven chapters and sixty articles. The government consisted of the governor, the congress and the court. People were granted democratic rights, the right to own private property, and the right to do business. The government decided that the 10th of October should be the national day for the Republic of China.

From the 18th of October to the 27th of November, the Revolutionary Army put up strong resistance against the army of the Qing government, which was massive. During those 41 days, most of the provinces declared their independence; only four provinces close to Peking, the capital (now called Beijing), still supported the Qing Dynasty. The governors of the independent provinces controlled the local army and became warlords.

All the independent provinces formed their own military governments. On the 1st of November, the Qing government appointed Yuan Shikai (1859–1916) premier. On the 1st of December, the Revolutionary Army and Yuan signed a truce. On the 2nd of December, the united army of Jiangsu and Zhejiang provinces occupied Nanking. On the 12th of December, representatives from all 14 independent provinces gathered in Nanking for a meeting. On the 17th of December, the representatives elected Li Yuanhong as the General Marshal and Huang Xing (1874–1916) as the Vice General Marshal.

On the 1ˢᵗ of January, 1912, the temporary government of the Republic of China established Nanking as its capital, breaking away from the Qing power base in Peking, and elected Sun Yat-sen as the temporary president.

Sun Yat-sen (The style of coat he's wearing is called Yat-sen coat.)

On the 12ᵗʰ of February, 1912, the last emperor of the Qing dynasty, Fu Yi (1906–1967, his English name: Henry) abdicated and the last dynasty ended, and with it ended the entire imperial system which had begun long ago and had lasted in much the same form for 2,000 years. But the imperial family still lived in the Forbidden City inside Peking.

The new republic had its national flag with five colors signifying the unity of five major tribes in China. They were the Han tribe, the Mandarin tribe, the Mongolian tribe, the Muslin tribe, and the Tibetan tribe, represented by horizontal bars of red, yellow, blue, white and black.

Flag of the first Republic of China

But the designs of the national flag for the Republic of China changed a few times, until the design was chosen which eventually became the national flag now still used in Taiwan: red background with a blue rectangle in the upper left corner, inside of which there is a 12-pointed white star, or sun.

The flag now used in Taiwan

With the establishment of the Republic of China, men cut off their queues, or braided pigtails, and wore short hair, more Western style. This style of shaving the front of the head and wearing the hair in a braid was originally imposed as a sign of submission demanded by the first Manchu Emperor. When they invaded the southern territories and occupied the lands of the Han tribe, they forced them to comply, too. If anyone refused to shave his front hair, he would be beheaded. The famous slogan was "Your hair or your head." For that reason, there had been a slaughter in Yangzhou city at that time, lasting for 10 days. Since the Revolution was victorious, now the pigtail had to go.

At the same time, women were freed of the custom of binding their feet; in fact, a major campaign was waged to discourage it. That custom had originated more than 1,000 years ago and affected all but the lowest workers, who could hardly afford to cripple themselves. (The Manchu Emperor had tried to ban it in 1664 but few paid any heed, as beauty, after all, comes at a price.) Now the revolution redefined some of the ideals of femininity and definitively freed women from the agony of crushing their feet.

The Qing Dynasty had persisted for almost 300 years. Why didn't it last longer? It was certainly not the fault of the last emperor, who was only three years old when he was put on the throne. The Qing Dynasty had degenerated over time, as most of them do, and corruption had grown worse and worse in the reign of Empress Dowager Cixi (1835–1908), his flamboyant grandmother, the subject of my earlier book *Empress Dowager Cixi* (Algora, 2002).

In the long history of China, two different women had managed to rule the country for tens of years. The first one was Empress Wu the Great, during the Tang Dynasty (AD 618–907). She read a great deal and trained herself as a politician and ruler. She ruled the country well (*Empress Wu the Great*, Algora, 2008). But Empress Dowager Cixi was no diplomat, no politician, and no wise ruler. She adopted wrong-headed policies. She came into power because of her status as the empress dowager. In her hands, the mansion of the great empire crumbled just like a house whose wooden beams and pillars are eaten through by white ants. The last emperor would not have been able to support it any more, no matter what.

The Ambition of Yuan Shikai

How Yuan became president of the Republic of China

When the Republic of China set its capital in Nanking on the 1st of January, 1912, Sun Yat-sen was elected temporary president and Li Yuanhong was elected vice president. At that time, the Emperor had not abdicated yet. The battle between the Revolutionary Army and the Qing army was still going on. The new army of the Qing government was organized and trained by Yuan Shikai (1859–1916), its commander. Yuan had a scheme of his own and began seeking a truce with the Revolutionary Army. Then he set his sights on the position of the President of the republic and forced the Emperor to abdicate.

Sun Yat-sen had no army that he himself had organized to support him. He had been elected temporary president owing to his reputation as a firm revolutionary against the Qing Dynasty. The Revolutionary Army was controlled by the governors (warlords) of the separate provinces; they signed an agreement with Yuan and refused to fight Yuan for Sun Yat-sen. Therefore, Sun Yat-sen had to give in. He resigned, and he nominated Yuan for president on the 15ᵗʰ of February. Accordingly, Yuan was named temporary president of the republic. As a rule, the president ought to live in the capital, which was Nanking, not Peking where Yuan lived. Yuan refused to come south because he could not bring his army south and would instead be controlled by the Revolutionary Army. After negotiations, the Revolutionary Army had to give in and let Yuan take office in Peking. But the congress was still in Nanking, controlled by the Nationalist Party.

In February 1913, the congress elected Song Jiaoren to be the Premier of the cabinet. At that time, Yuan had Zhao Binjun as his premier. However, on the 20ᵗʰ of March, Song was assassinated at the railway station in Shanghai. When the assassin was caught, evidence on his person linked him to Zhao—actual letters between Zhao and the assassin, no less. So the Nationalist Party drew the conclusion that Yuan was behind it. Zhao resigned under pressure from the press. Duan Qirui (1865–1936) was appointed to take over the office of the premier.

After the assassination, Sun Yat-sen, who was at the time on a visit in Japan, came back to Shanghai and summoned a meeting of the Nationalist Party. He suggested avenging Yuan with armed force, though some other leaders like Huang Xing tended to appeal to less violent conduct.

On the 26ᵗʰ of April, Yuan asked for a syndicate loan of 25 million British pounds from the lending consortium in China consisting of England, France, Germany, Russia and Japan. The Nationalist Party thought that the loan request was illegal, as it would require approval by the congress first. In May, Li Liejun, the governor of Jiangxi province, Hu Hanming, the governor of Guangdong province, and Bo Wenwei, the governor of Anhui province, declared their opposition to the loan. The three governors were all members of the Nationalist Party. In June, Yuan gave orders to remove the three from their positions as governors. On the 3ʳᵈ of July, Yuan sent the sixth division of his new army to Jiangxi province.

Under instructions from Sun Yat-sen, Li Liejun declared the independence of Jiangxi province on the 12ᵗʰ of the same month, and formed a separate headquarters from which to oppose Yuan. On the 15th, Huang Xing reached Nanking and declared the independence of Jiangsu province. Quite a few provinces followed suit.

On the 22nd of July, the Nationalist Army from Jiangsu province fought a battle with Yuan's army at Xuzhou of Shandong province and was defeated. The Nationalist Army was conquered in some other places, too. Then all the independent provinces had to rescind their declarations of independence. Yuan issued orders to arrest Sun Yat-sen and Huang Xing, who had already escaped to Japan. This event was called the Second Revolution, but it ended in failure.

On the 6th of October, the congress held a session in Peking and the congressmen were forced to elect Yuan Shikai as president and Li Yuanhong as vice president of the republic. Yuan took the official oath on the 10th of October.

Yuan Shikai as president of first Republic of China. Yuan wanted to be the new emperor

On the 4th of November, Yuan Shikai gave an order to disband the Nationalist Party, using their rebellion as a pretext. Simultaneously, he drove all the members of the Nationalist Party out of the congress. On the 10th of January, 1914, Yuan dismissed the congress entirely and formed his own council of state, which meant that all the members were his men. He was still dissatisfied with being president. He wanted to be emperor.

To attain his goal, he first had to get international support. In January of 1915, Japan secretly gave Yuan a document containing 21 articles in 5 chapters, through which China should cede to Japan a variety of economic and commercial rights and benefits, such as options on railroads and other profitable fields in Manchuria, and in Shandong province, and also the extension of Japan's occupation of Luushun and Dalian (two harbor cities) to 99 years, etc. But two articles in particular were unacceptable. One was to employ Japanese advisors in the Chinese central government, in the financial and military fields. The other was to employ Japanese advisors in local police departments. The negotiations ran from the 2nd of February to the 7th of May.

Yuan Shikai accepted most of the articles in order to secure Japan's support for his ambition to be emperor. But such a big secret could not be kept for long and soon the public heard that he was selling them out. Yuan was severely criticized, but to no avail.

Then Yuan Shikai's supporters began to circulate their theory that the republican form of government was not suitable to China. They formed a committee on the political future of China and sent out their men to all the provinces to persuade officials and officers and businessmen to support Yuan as emperor, promising all of them personal benefits. Then such supporters were summoned to the capital as "people's representatives." Those representatives formed groups and on the 1st of September handed a petition to the Council of State (organized by Yuan) to ask Yuan to be the emperor.

In a traditional show of modesty, Yuan Shikai initially refused their petition. On the 19th, they organized the "National Petition Committee" to turn in a second petition, this time requesting that the 1993 people's representatives should hold a conference to decide the future of the nation. Accordingly, the conference was in session at 9 o'clock in the morning on December 11. The representatives were to cast votes. All the representatives voted for the imperial system. Yuan graciously accepted the result as the supposed will of the people, and decided that the next year (1916) would be the first year of his Empire of China.

Flag of Yuan Shikai's China Empire

In December, just after Yuan Shikai accepted the petition, Cai E, the governor of Yunnan province, was the first to object. Yunnan is in the mountains, at the border with Vietnam, Laos and Burma, and the population includes many non-Han people. He announced the independence of Yunnan, followed by many provinces. Even Yuan's former subordinates, Feng Guozhang (1859–1916), governor of Jiangsu province, Li Chun, governor of Jiangxi province, Zhu Rui, governor of Zhejiang province, Jin Yunpeng, governor of Shandong province, and Tang Xiangming, governor of Hunan province, all sent telegrams asking Yuan Shikai to rescind his declaration of the empire.

Seeing that even his former subordinates had betrayed him, Yuan Shikai had to declare openly that he was restoring the presidency on the 22nd of March, 1916. He had been Emperor only for 83 days. Once a high military official of the Qing Dynasty, he had turned against the empire, and then he was subverted in turn. He contracted a fatal disease and died on the 6th of June.

If he had not been so ambitious and had contented himself with the presidency, Yuan would have been spared the hatred of almost all the people in China. He would not have been betrayed by his closest generals, who commanded part of his new army. But he went against the historical tide, against the will of people. He wanted to turn back time to the imperial age. As a president, his subordinates only had to stand up before him and salute him, whereas during his heady days as emperor, his subordinates had to kneel before him and kowtow to him. Any man who has had a chance to stand up never wants to bend his knees again. Sense of dignity.

There would have to be a public funeral for Yuan. According to the law, when the president died, the vice president would succeed him. So Li Yuanhong became the president. Also, as a rule, the public funeral for a deceased president should be led by the succeeding president. But Li Yuanhong had a little problem with Yuan Shikai, for Yuan had sent Li to prison. That made it rather hard for Li to feign any esteem for Yuan. So on the day of the funeral, he just went there to bow once and left, back to his office. As etiquette required, he should have bowed at least three times. Then the Premier Duan Qirui took over the role.

Chaos

Restoration of the abdicated emperor

Li Yuanhong and Duan Qirui had also clashed. Their opinions and political attitudes were different. As Li had no supporters in the government, Duan had no respect for him. Duan also had command of part of the new army. So Li sought support outside the capital.

In May of 1917, during the First World War, there was a dispute about whether China would join in the war or not. Duan Qirui, supported by Japan, was in favor of joining the war, while Li Yuanhong and most of the congressmen thought it better not to join the war. On the 23rd of May, Li issued an order to remove Duan Qirui from the office of premier. Duan went to Tainjin City and instigated all the governors to declare independence. So Li summoned General Zhang Xun (1854–1923) to the capital to mediate.

Zhang Xun was still loyal to the Qing Dynasty and the soldiers in his army still maintained their queues. So his army was called the pigtail army. He thought that this was a great opportunity and took five thousand soldiers with him. On the 14th of June, he entered Peking. On the night of the 30th of June, he sent his soldiers to occupy strategic points like the railway station and telegraph office. He went to see Li and tried to persuade him to return the political power to the abdicated Emperor Puyi, by now using the Western name of Henry, but got a flat refusal.

On the 1st of July, 1917, Zhang Xun let the abdicated emperor sit on the throne again and issue a few orders, such as to change the national flag from the five-colored flag (the symbol of Republic of China) to dragon flag (the symbol of the Qing Dynasty).

On the 2nd of July, Li went to the Japanese embassy for protection while issuing two orders: appointing Feng Guozhang as the deputy president and restored Duan to the office of the premier. So on the 3rd of July, Duan gathered his army, and on the 14th day, he defeated Zhang Xun's pigtail army. Zhang Xun escaped to the Dutch embassy, then went to live in Tianjin City. The Emperor abdicated once more. And Duan went to the Japanese embassy to welcome Li back to his presidency. On the 28th of August, Li went to Tianjin City after resigning.

Thus, in the early history of the Republic of China, there were two restorations. One was under Yuan Shikai, who wanted to be emperor himself and founded the Empire of China. The other was Zhang Xun, who put the abdicated emperor on the throne again. But both quickly ended in failure. The chariot of history always runs forward and no one can pull it back. People won't go back to the old life style once they start to enjoy a new one, especially one that offers more freedom and dignity.

As Li Yuanhong resigned from the presidency, the deputy president Feng Guozhang became the president. Feng was the governor of Jiangsu province and lived in Nanking. Now he was the president and had to take up office in Peking. That left the position of governor of Jiangsu province vacant. Duan Qirui wanted to appoint Duan Zhigui as the governor there, but Feng wanted to appoint Li Chun, the present governor of Jiangxi province as the governor of Jiangsu province. He promoted Chen Guangyuan, who was the commander of the twelfth division, to be the governor of Jiangxi province. Both were supporters of Feng. Before he left for Peking, he divided his army into two divisions. The sixteenth division would stay in Jiangsu province. He brought his fifteenth division to Peking as his bodyguard so that he wouldn't be controlled by Duan.

Duan dismissed the old congress because most of the congressmen had opposed him on the question of joining in the First World War. Since there was no more congress, the Duan government declared war against Germany and Austria.

May 4 student movement

On the 23rd of August, 1914, Japan declared war against Germany and took over Jiaozhou Bay in Shandong province, formerly occupied by Germany. They fought for 70 days. Then in January 1915, Japan had put the 21 articles to Yuan, who accepted most of them. These were considered a national insult, which caused great dissatisfaction with the government among Chinese intellectuals, including university students.

China declared war against Germany on the 14th of August, 1917, actually at the end of the First World War, so that China was one of the victorious countries. But at the Paris Peace Conference, which produced the Versailles Treaty, Japan was allowed to continue its occupation of Jiaozhou Bay, which should have been returned to China since it was in the territory of China and formerly was occupied by Germany.

The public called upon the Chinese representative at the conference to refuse to sign on the treaty, but the government secretly instructed the representative to go ahead and sign it. When the news became openly known, the students at Peking University held an emergency meeting on the 1st of May. On the night of the 3rd day, students from other universities joined in the action. They decided to hold a demonstration on TianAnMen Square on the 4th of May, which was Sunday. Thus began the May 4 movement.

At one o'clock in the afternoon, the students marched towards the neighborhood where all the embassies were and distributed copies of a memorandum, which was refused by all the embassies except the American one. Then they went to the residence of Cao Rulin, minister of transportation (to complain about the railway problem with Japan), where they saw Zhang Zongxiang, the Chinese ambassador to Japan. The students gave both a good beating and set fire to the residence. For that, 32 students were arrested.

To rescue the students, the professors called on the public

to declare a strike of all students, teachers, workers, and shop-owners. The government forbade it and arrested more people. The chaos lasted into June; people answered the call of the professors and the movement spread to many cities. Even railway workers started to strike. On the 11th of June, Professor Chen Duxiu (1879–1942) and others distributed pamphlets in public, and Chen was arrested. The chaos worsened. Under such pressure, the government had to give in. It dismissed Cao and Zhang from office and released those in jail. On the 28th of June, the representative attending the Paris Peace Conference did not sign the treaty.

This movement was influential not only in politics, but also in culture. Many changes were introduced. Professor Hu Shih proposed that language as spoken should be used in writing instead of the classical language. Hence, the language style in use was changed, even in newspapers. So the May 4 movement is also called the new cultural movement.

Battles in the southwestern provinces

Chinese historians define the men who command independent armies as warlords. In many periods this included the governors of provinces, and even premiers like Duan Qirui, who had his own army. The local warlords often disobeyed the central government. If the central government wanted any governor to obey its orders, it had to send an army to defeat him. And the provincial governors often fought one another to increase their power base. As a result, many periods of history were fraught with turmoil.

Although Yuan Shikai died, his former supporters controlled most provinces. Only five provinces in southwestern China were under the influence of the Nationalist Party. They were Yunnan, Sichuan, Guizhou, Guangdong and Guangxi provinces.

In Sichuan province there were three armies. One came from Yunnan province. One came from Guizhou province. And the third one was formed of local soldiers. Each of them wanted to take control of Sichuan province and they fought one another from time to time. Premier Duan of the central government wanted to control this province, too. So he sent a detachment of his army to Sichuan province. Then, the three local armies united to fight against Duan Qirui's army, which had to retreat.

After the failure of the second revolution, Sun Yat-sen endeavored to make another attempt. He gained the support of the Navy's First Fleet. In 1917, the governor of Guangdong province proposed to Sun that he could use this province as his headquarters against the warlord government in Peking. On the 10th of July, Sun took two warships to Shantou Town and sent Zhang Binglin to Guangdong province as his representative. The situation in that province was complicated, though. On the 17th, when Sun arrived in Canton on board a warship, he was welcomed. On the 22nd day, the commander of the First Fleet brought his fleet to Guangdong province, too. They announced that since the dismissal of the Congress, any orders from the Peking government were unlawful.

When Duan learned the news, he promoted the commander of the Second Fleet to be the commander of the navy and appointed another admiral as commander of the First Fleet, which was not under his control any more. On the 25th day Duan ordered to remove the governor of Guangdong province from office, but the governor refused to recognize the order.

Sun Yat-sen invited the congressmen to come south. In mid-August, more than 130 congressmen arrived in Canton. On the 18th, at a welcome party, all the attendees agreed to organize a new military government, which was founded on the 10th of September. When Duan Qirui heard of this, he issued a "wanted" bulletin for Sun Yat-sen, and the military government also issued a "wanted" bulletin for Duan. The five provinces in the southeastern China supported the military government against Duan, who sent his army into Hunan province in hopes of defeating the army of the military government.

On the 6th of October, two armies engaged in battle near Xiangtan Town. Contrary to Duan's hopes, his army was forced to withdraw. It looked bad for him, and many provinces announced their support for the military government. Duan had to resign as premier.

President Feng called upon both sides to stop fighting. Duan had always been a threat to the independent governors in the southeastern region, and now they felt that the sword of Damocles had been removed, so they agreed to the truce. But on the 2nd of December, 1917, Duan instigated ten northern gover-nors to take action against the southeastern provinces. On the 6th, they pressed President Feng to issue orders to continue the war. Meanwhile, Zhang Zuolin, the warlord in the northeastern China, led his army into Peking. Under such pressure, Feng had to ask Duan to resume the office of premier.

Duan re-organized his army to attack the army of the mili-tary government, which now lost the support of the other gover-nors and had to fight alone. It was soon defeated. But Wu Peifu (1874–1939), the commander of Duan's army, ceased his assault and made a truce with the military government, ignoring Duan's command. As Feng and Duan always had conflicts of opinion, or in reality, of personal interests, both agreed to resign at the same time. That was on the 4th of September, 1918.

Sun Yat-sen's goal was to let his National Party unite the whole of China under the rule of his party. But this ran counter to the interests of the warlords. So he lost most of his supporters and only a few were left. On the 21st of May, 1918, he left Canton for Shanghai, where he met Chiang Kai-shek (1887–1975). The military government was controlled by the armies of Yunnan and Guangxi provinces.

As Sun resigned and left Canton, his army (under the com-mand of Chen Jiongming) went to Fujian province, and together with the army under the command of Chiang Kai-shek they de-feated Duan's army there. That happened in June of 1918.

Although Duan Qirui was not in the cabinet, he still had his army. So Zhang Zuoling (1875–1928) and Wu Peifu allied to fight him. On the 14th of July, 1920, Duan's army was overcome. Then Xu Shichang, who had nothing under his control, was selected (not elected, as there was no more congress) by the warlords to be a puppet president.

In August 1920, the army stationed in Fujian province marched back to Guangdong province to assail the Guangxi province army there. On the 28th of October, the military govern-ment was back under the control of Sun's army. So on the 28th of November, Sun returned to Canton.

On the 12th of January, 1921, a special congress was organized and on the 2nd of April, the congress held a session to annul the military government and resume the name of the Republic of

China. On the 7th day, Sun was elected President and took an oath at a ceremony on the 5th of May.

Sun Yat-sen goes north, looking to overthrow the Peking government

Sun Yat-sen still persisted in marching north to overthrow the Peking government. He thought of it as a warlord government, not a revolutionary government. He wanted to found a revolutionary government for the people. Anyway, the governors of all the provinces and even Chen Jiongming (1878–1933), the commander of his army (actually another warlord), did not see things that way. Those men only wanted to have a federal government of warlords.

On the 26th of March, 1922, Sun Yat-sen held a meeting and decided to go north to take down the Peking government. On the 9th of April, when the Revolutionary Army reached the Meng River, it was blockaded by Chen Jiongming's army which was encamped there. Sun gave orders that if Chen's army did not make way for him, he would launch an attack. When Sun reached Wuzhou Town, he summoned Chen Jiongming to meet him, but Chen refused to go there. Sun removed him from the position of commander. Chen wanted his army to prepare for a war against Sun, but the army in Canton refused to carry out his order. There was nothing he could do but go back to his old home in Huizhou Town. However, part of his army was still loyal to him.

In early April 1922, Wu Peifu sent an emissary to contact Chen Jiongming and asked him to prevent Sun Yat-sen by force from going north. Meantime, Duan and Zhang Zuolin wanted to ally with Sun to vanquish Wu. The situation got complicated. Everyone was putting his own interests first and relationships between friends and enemies often changed.

On the 23rd of April, Sun Yat-sen gathered his generals for a meeting in his presidential residence to decide what to do next. There were two options. One was to first annihilate Chen Jiongming's army so that he could not give the Revolutionary Army a stab from behind. Chiang Kai-shek held this opinion. The other was to immediately march north, while doing their best to avoid any conflict with Chen's army. Sun tended toward the second opinion, as he thought that Chen Jiongming had not really betrayed him, at least not yet. He had no reason to attack Chen. Chiang Kai-shek thought that Chen would at long last betray Sun. Since Sun did not believe him, he left Guangdong province, while writing a letter to Chen advising him not to betray Sun.

When Sun Yat-sen came back to Canton, he still allowed Chen to be the commander of the first army. But Chen refused to take the appointment. On the 28th of April, Zhang Zuolin, Duan Qirui and Sun Yat-sen formed an alliance to fight Wu Peifu. Sun thought that this created an opportunity for him to go north.

On the 4th of May, Zhang's army was beaten by Wu Peifu's, and Zhang had to retreat back to where he had come from, northeastern China. Wu took control in Peking. Wu had a secret agreement with Chen Jiongming that he would drive away the current president, Xu Shichang, and Chen would drive away Sun Yat-sen. Then the first step was to let Li Yuanhong back into the presidency and get him to wipe out all the warlords everywhere, except of course the two of them. If Li failed to do so, he would be the scapegoat. If he succeeded, Wu and Chen would use the congress to have themselves elected as the president and the vice president.

So they announced that the current president Xu was illegal. Xu resigned on the 2nd of June. Once back in the presidency, Li denounced that warrant that was out for Sun Yat-sen and invited him to Peking to discuss national affairs. He also appointed many warlords in the south, but none of them accepted his appointments. Afterwards, as Wu and Chen saw that Li could do nothing for them, they forced Li to quit the presidency again. Li went back to Tianjin City.

On the 9th of May, Sun issued an order for a general attack, and on the 13th of June, the Revolutionary Army put Wu's army to rout in Jiangxi province. Wu sent his man to Chen and asked him to take action as soon as possible.

Chen Jiongming turns traitor in Canton

When Chen Jiongming went back to his hometown, he took with him a lot of guns and ammunition, enough to arm 40 battalions. On the 20th of May, Chen's subordinate, Ye Ju, led his troops into Canton and started a treasonous action. By the 1st of

June, the situation had become acute. Liao Zhongkai, a faithful follower of Sun, sent a telegram to Sun Yat-sen asking him to come back to Canton. When Sun was back in Canton, he summoned Chen, but Chen refused to come.

On the 12th of June, Sun Yat-sen ordered Ye Ju out of Canton. Next day, Chen Jiongming and Ye secretly met at Shilong. They knew that, to prevent Sun from going north to fight Wu Peifu, they would have to cut off his access to financing. Liao was the person who provided Sun with everything, so they decided to kidnap Liao. On the 14th day, Chen sent a telegram Liao to invite him to his hometown for some important business. On the fifth day, Liao went there and was detained. Then Ye Ju maneuvered his troops and planned to attack Sun's residence with cannons. On the 16th day, Sun was informed of this and took refuge on a warship.

On the 19th, Sun Yat-sen sent a telegram to the Revolutionary Army at the front to come back to Guangdong province. On the 2nd of July, the Revolutionary Army started to assail Chen Jiongming's army in Guangdong province, and beat the betraying army. Chen sent a telegram to Wu seeking assistance. Wu sent some troops to Guangdong province. On the 26th of July, the Revolutionary Army was chasing after Chen's retreating army but met with the reinforcements sent by Wu. Therefore, the Revolutionary Army had to withdraw. When Sun Yat-sen learned this, he had to leave Guangdong province and go to Shanghai. Liao was released and left Canton. When Chen attempted to assassinate him afterwards, he was already gone.

On the 16th of August, 1922, Sun Yat-sen made a statement accusing Chen of betrayal. To annihilate the treacherous army, Sun determined to ally with Duan. In October, he appointed Xu Chongzhi as the commander-in-chief and Chiang Kai-shek as the chief of staff. On one side, the Revolutionary Army together with Duan's army vanquished Wu's army. On the other, the armies of Yunnan and Guangxi provinces, who supported Sun, defeated Chen's army. On the 14th of January, 1923, troops in Guangdong province turned over to Sun and attacked Chen, who escaped to his hometown, Huizhou.

On the 15th of February, Sun Yat-sen returned to Canton. In April, Chen Hongying, a warlord in Guangxi province, accepted the appointment of the Peking government to be the governor of Guangdong province, and came to attack Canton, but was soon subdued. He escaped to Hong Kong.

In January of 1925, Sun went to Peking to discuss national affairs, but he was fatally ill. In February the Revolutionary Army, now under the full command of Chiang Kai-shek, marched east to wipe out the warlords there. Sun died on the 12th of March. He famously wrote, in his will, "The revolution is not successful yet; comrades must still make efforts." That June, Chen Jiongming betrayed the cause again, but he was soon wiped out by Chiang Kai-shek.

Early History of the Communist Party of China

The organization of the Communist Party of China

In April 1920, the Communist International sent Grigori Voitinsky to China. In May, he found Chen Duxiu, 42 at the time, and sought to contact some revolutionary young men in other cities to establish the Communist Party of China, the CPC. Chen Duxiu was the professor mentioned above who had been arrested in the May 4 student movement in 1919. In August 1920, under instructions of the Soviet Communist Party, the Communist Party of China was established.

But public data state that the first meeting of the Communist Party was held about a year later, in Shanghai, on the 1st of July, 1921. Why was the earlier date concealed from the public? There might be two reasons. One was that they wanted to cover up the fact that the Communist International had had a hand in it. The other is that Mao attended the meeting in Shanghai, so by emphasizing that meeting they could say that Mao was one of the founders, enhancing his image. But the meeting was in 1920, not in 1921 in Shanghai.

Fifteen people attended the meeting on the 23rd of July, 1921, at 106 Wangzhi Road (presently 76 Xingye Road) in Shanghai. These included Mao Zedong (1893–1976); Dong Biwu (1886–1975), later the vice chairman of the People's Republic of China); Zhang Guotao (1897–1979), later commander of the Red 4th Army in the Long March); Chen Gongbo (1890–1946); and Zhou Fohai (1897–1948). The last two later defected to the Japanese invaders during the Sino–Japanese War (1937—1945). Also present were Malin and Nico Chhabra (representatives from the Communist International).

Soon some suspicious men were found lurking outside the house. The meeting broke up and everyone discretely slipped away. And the next day, they met on a boat on the South Lake in Jiaxing Town, casually playing mahjong while in fact continuing their meeting. Thus the Communist Party of China was established. At that time it had only 50 members.

On the 23rd of December, 1921, accompanied by an interpreter, Malin went to see Sun Yat-sen in Guilin City of Guangxi province. He stayed there for nine days and concluded that Communist Party members could join the Nationalist Party while still maintaining their status in the Communist Party. This would help the Communist Party to develop. But his idea was strongly opposed by some party members, especially Chen Duxiu who was then the leader of the party. So on the 23rd of April, 1922, Malin left Shanghai for Holland, by sea, and then, through Berlin, made it to Moscow. He reported his work in China to the Soviet Communist Party, which consented to his idea. On the 27th of July, the Soviet Union sent a representative to China, together with Malin, with instructions. Malin typed the instructions on the shirt he wore. In Shanghai, Malin met Chen Duxiu and gave him his shirt.

Chen DuXiu had to obey the decision of the Communist International because at the second meeting of the Communist Party, held from July 16–23, 1922, at 625 South Chengdu Road in Shanghai, they had decided to join the Communist International. Chen Duxiu and Zhang Guotao attended the meeting with ten other representatives. Then the Communist Party of China got financial aid from the Communist International.

On the 29th and 30th of August, 1922, the Communist Party of China (CPC) held a central meeting on the West Lake in Hangzhou City and decided to found the First United Front, an alliance between the Nationalist Party and the Communist Party.

The next year, from in June 1923, the Communist Party had its third meeting in Canton, and 40 representatives, representing 420 party members, discussed the issue of the First United Front. They elected Chen Duxiu, Li Dazhao (1889–1927), Mao

Zedong, and Xiang Ying (1898–1941) who later became commander of the New 4th Army in the Sino–Japanese War), and five others, as members of the Central Committee.

It was said that after the meeting, at the urging of the Communist Party, Sun Yat-sen proposed his three great policies: Alliance with Russia, Co-operation with the Communist Party, and Assistance to Peasants and Workers. But as a matter of fact, Sun never identified with such policies. This was just invented by Mikhail Markovich Borodin, a Russian counselor to the Communist Party of China, to make them look good. Then the Communist Party used this invention as a fact for its own purposes.

Why did Sun agree to the United Front notion? It was because Sun always held to his ideal of Three Principles for the People: the Principle of Nationalism, the Principle of Democracy, and the Principle of People's Livelihood. Ironically, this party, the "Kuomintang" in Chinese, evolved into a highly centralized, hierarchical, and authoritarian party. Sun thought that the ideal of communism was closest to his three principles and so he wanted to unite with the Communist Party against their common enemies—warlords who were still taking advantage of the power void left when the imperial order crumbled.

From the 20th to the 30th of January, 1924, the 196 representatives of the Nationalist Party held their first conference in Canton (now Guangzhou). Sun was the chairman and the Russian counselor Borodin was in attendance. Some Communist Party members were elected into the executive committee of the Nationalist Party. Li Dazhao and a few others were members and Mao Zedong, Zhang Guotao were alternate members.

In the autumn of 1924, General Feng Yuxiang (1882–1948) launched a coup d'état and took control of the Peking government. He invited Sun Yat-sen to Peking to discuss national affairs. In the morning of November 5, Feng sent his troops to surround the Forbidden City and ordered the abdicated emperor to move out. So Henry gathered his precious belongings and moved to Tianjin City with his family. A few faithful old courtiers followed him there.

On November 13, Sun Yat-sen arrived in Peking. It was soon found that he was suffering from liver cancer and he died on March 12, 1925. Sun had been in Peking three times. First, in

1894, he went to Peking with the intention of advising the Qing officials on how it might reform the government. But when he saw how serious the corruption was, he realized that no reform could be enough to save China. So he decided to make a revolution. His second visit was in 1912 when the Republic of China was founded. He went to Peking to advise Yuan Shikai that if Yuan could carry on the revolution, he would resign from the temporary presidency. This was his third time.

On the 15th of September, Zhang Zuolin came with his forces from the northeastern provinces towards Peking and allied with Feng Yuxiang. Then a battle broke out between Zhang, Feng and Wu Peifu. Wu's army was put to rout and Wu escaped south to Hunan and Hubei provinces. Thereafter, Peking fell under the control of Zhang Zuolin, who was always backed by Japan.

Whampoa military academy

The Whampoa Military Academy was founded on the 16th of June, 1924, on the instruction of Sun Yat-sen, to train officers for the Revolutionary Army. It was situated on Changzhou Island in the Whampoa District of Canton. Afterwards, branches were founded in Wuhan, Changsha, Chaoshan, and Nanning cities. In preparation for the establishment of this academy, Sun had sent Chiang Kai-shek to the Soviet Union in September of 1923 to learn from their experience. So the academy was modeled after those in the Soviet Union. And Chiang Kai-shek was appointed President of the academy. Quite a few Communist Party (CPC) members were appointed leaders of departments, such as Ye Jianying (1897–1986), deputy director of the training department, and Zhou Enlai (1898–1976), deputy director of the political department.

In May of 1924, the academy began to take in students. Out of 1200 applicants, 350 students were enrolled and 120 were accepted as alternate students for the first term. In 1927, the academy was relocated in Nanking and renamed the Central Army Officer Academy. Later, in 1949, it moved to Taiwan, for reasons that will become apparent later. From 1924 to 1949, there were 23 terms, and including the terms held in Taiwan, the academy was functioning for 78 terms. The academy graduated 41,386 students, including many famous generals.

The Break-up of the Nationalist Party and the Communist Party

After the death of Sun Yat-sen, Chiang Kai-shek took the full command of the Revolutionary Army. Unlike Sun Yat-sen, Chiang Kai-shek had no confidence in the CPC, especially after their fourth conference.

That fourth conference of the Communist Party was held from the 11th to the 22nd of January, 1925, with 20 representatives gathered in Shanghai. Chen Duxiu, Zhang Guotao, Zhou Enlai, and Xiang Ying, and many others attended. Chen was the chairman. During the conference, Chen was elected the general secretary of the central bureau, consisting of five persons. They decided that the Communist Party had to take charge of the revolution, and that laid the ground for major disruptions.

On the 20th of March, 1926, the warship *Yat-sen* planned an artillery attack on the Whanpoa Military Academy to drive away Chiang Kai-shek. Chiang gave orders to arrest the captain, Li Zhilong, a member of the Communist Party. Then Chiang ordered Zhou Enlai and all their party members to get out of the academy. The students now faced a problem as to which party they would follow. One student quit the Nationalist Party and 39 students quit the Communist Party. The others remained in the academy.

Meanwhile within the Nationalist Party, Wang Jingwei (1883–1944), who later treacherously went over to the Japanese during the Sino–Japanese War) wanted to take over the leadership of the Nationalist Party. He organized another government in Wuhan City, close to Wuchang City, the cradle of the 1911 revolution, and held the third conference of the Nationalist Party without the attendance of Chiang. This was called Wuhan government.

At that time Chiang only had command of the Revolution Army and held no position in the government. The Wuhan government wanted Chiang to continue to the north to wipe out the warlords there. But Chiang planned to go east to occupy the eastern provinces first, including Shanghai, because those eastern provinces were also under the control of warlords.

During those years, the land problem was serious. Peasants

wanted to have their own land so that they would not be exploited by landowners. When peasants worked land owned by those in the ownership class, they had to give part of the harvest to the landowners, as in any feudal system. As the imperial system had been demolished, they wanted land reforms too. Under instigation by the Communist Party, they began to demand this more and more aggressively.

Stalin, head of the Soviet Union, asked the Communist Party of China in October of 1926 to curb the action of peasants, to reduce the violence. In March of 1927, the Communist Party established legal penalties for landowners. Any landowners who resisted the revolution would be put to death.

On the 2nd of April, 1927, the Central Committee of the Nationalist Party held a meeting in Wuhan, inviting two members of the Communist Party, one of whom was Mao Zedong. They were considering a bill about the land problem. The government would confiscate the land of "reactionaries" (those who preferred the old ways as opposed to the revolution) such as property owners, officials who had a stake in the old system, and warlords. The definition of reactionary landowners was to be based on the amount of land they owned, measured by the mu (about 0.165 acres). Anyone who had more than 30 mus, about 5 acres, was dubbed a reactionary. All landowners would be classified into rich peasants, small and middle landowners, and large landowners, according to the amount of terrain they possessed. This standard was still used in the land reform when the Communist Party later established their republic.

On the 22nd of April, when this bill was under discussion, the Nationalist Party and the CPC had different opinions. That was one of the reasons for their falling out, because many members of the Nationalist Party came from families who owned land. Then on the 26th of April, Chen Duxiu and Zhang Guotao were invited to attend the meeting, and also Borodin, the Russian counselor. On the 6th of May, the bill was at last passed. Only the large landowners would see their land confiscated. The land belonging to small landowners and families of revolutionary officials would remain the same. However, once the peasants had been instigated, it was hard to check their zeal to take possession of the land.

Victory of the Revolutionary Army and the final break between the two parties

In July of 1926, the Nationalist Party decided the Revolutionary Army should head north to annihilate the warlords there. As Chiang was the commander-in-chief, he led the army north, fighting all the way along the route. The plan was for the Revolutionary Army to attack Wu Peifu first, and then Sun Chuanfang, occupying Jiangxi, Fujian, Anhui, Jiangsu, and Zhejiang, five provinces. Finally the Revolutionary Army would attack Zhang Zuolin in Peking.

In August of 1926, the Revolutionary Army assaulted the main force of Wu Peifu and wiped it out; they took over Wuchang city on the 10ᵗʰ of September. In November, the Revolutionary Army annihilated the main force of Sun Chuanfang, another warlord, and occupied Jiujiang and Nanchang cities. At the same time, Feng Yuxiang gained control of the northwestern region of China. A warlord, Yan Xishan (1883–1960), ruled Shanxi province. Observing the rapid advance of the Revolutionary Army, both Feng and Yan joined it. Now only the warlord Zhang Zuolin from the northeastern provinces remained in Peking.

In October, the Communist Party organized workers in Shanghai to rise to arms against the warlord government 675 miles north in Peking, but they failed. In November, the Revolutionary Army took control of the area of the Yangtze River. So the Nationalist Government decided to establish its capital in Wuhan City, but Chiang wanted the capital in Nanchang, which was then under his control. Anyway, on the 9ᵗʰ of December, the Nationalist Government moved to Wuhan City.

On the 21ˢᵗ of February, 1927, the Central Committee of the Nationalist Party held a meeting of the 80 members, one third belonged to the Communist Party and one third were communist-leaning. Among the leaders of all the departments of the Nationalist Party, half of them were members of the Communist Party. This meant that the CPC controlled the Nationalist Party. And the Communist Party was organizing its own army.

Chiang Kai-shek decided he had to found another government. He had many supporters, like the brothers Chen Guofu (1892–1951) and Chen Lifu (1900–2001) and others in his army. All were young men.

On the 19th of February, General Bai Chongxi (1893–1966) took over Hangzhou city as he marched east with his detachment of the Revolutionary Army. On the 22nd, the Communist Party fomented a second riot in Shanghai but failed once more. On the 10th of March, the Central Committee of the Nationalist Party had another meeting to openly declare their break with Chiang, and he cut off all relations with the Communist Party.

Then Wang Jingwei came back from France, where he attended classes in the University of Lyon, and reorganized the Nationalist Party by expelling the Russian counselor and members of the Communist Party. He also suggested that the Nationalist government and the headquarters of the Nationalist Party be moved to Nanking.

On the 22nd of March, the east detachment of the Revolutionary Army under Bai Chongxi entered Shanghai. On the 24th, the middle detachment occupied Nanking. A few members of the Communist Party instigated the soldiers of the Revolutionary Army to rob and kill foreigners in order to incite foreign governments to take action against the Nationalist government. But the consuls of England, the United States and Japan had evidence that the Communist Party was responsible for the trouble.

On the fifth of April, the Central Committee of the Nationalist Party divided the Revolutionary Army into two military blocs. Chiang was re-appointed the commander-in-chief of the first military bloc and Feng Yuxiang was the commander-in-chief of the second. On the same day, Chiang contacted the heads of certain mafias in Shanghai and asked them to organize a Shanghai business guild to oppose the Shanghai workers' general union, an armed group which was controlled by the Communist Party.

Meantime, Borodin secretly urged General Guo Songling under the warlord government to fight Zhang Zuolin, who had secret contacts with Chiang. On the 6th of April, Zhang suddenly attacked the embassy of the Soviet Union in Peking to arrest 58 members of the Communist Party hiding there, including Li Dazhao, one of the main founders of the Communist Party. They found secret documents which proved that the Soviet Union instructed the Communist Party to overthrow the Chinese government. On the 12th of April, Chiang sent the national 26th army to the Shanghai workers' general union to order them to surrender their weapons. But they refused, and many people were killed in the conflict, which became known as the 4/12 event. Then Chiang ordered all the organizations controlled by the Communist Party to disband.

On the 17th of April, Chiang and other members of the Central Committee of the Nationalist Party met in Nanking to issue warrant for the arrest of 197 leading members of the Communist Party, including Borodin, Chen Duxiu, Mao Zedong, Zhou Enlai, Liu Shaoqi (1898–1969), Zhang Guotao, Deng Yingchao (1904–1992, wife of Zhou Enlai), and others. On the 28th, Li Dazhao and others were hanged in Peking, accused of plotting to overthrow the government.

On the 20th of April, the Communist Party issued a statement saying that Chiang was the open foe of the revolutionary people and called upon the people to overthrow him. On the 22nd day, Wang Jingwei and other members of the Nationalist Party who supported the Communist Party, together with Mao Zedong and some Communist Party members, openly blamed Chiang for the disruption. Chiang founded the Nationalist government in Nanking in opposition to the government in Wuhan City.

On the fifth of June when Indian revolutionary M.N. Roy, a representative of the Communist International, asked Wang Jingwei to allow the Communist Party to control the Wuhan government, Wang began to disband the Communist Party. Therefore, on the 1st of August, the Communist Party called for riots in Nanchang. That marked the final rupture between the Nationalist Party and the Communist Party.

CHAPTER 2. THE FIRST CIVIL WAR BETWEEN THE NATIONALIST PARTY AND THE COMMUNIST PARTY

Communist Party Riots

The riot in Nanchang City

Wang Jingwei learned that the Soviet Union was planning to help the Communist Party of China to take over power from Wuhan government in July 1927. He expelled all the members of the Communist Party that were in the Nationalist Party and the Wuhan government. This led the Central Committee of the Communist Party in Jiujiang city (Jiangxi province) to foment a riot in Nanchang city, where they controlled some of the army. On the 26th of July, Zhou Enlai was sent to organize the riot. Several hours after Zhou left, they got a telegram from the Communist International, instructing them not to start it if there was no chance of winning. So Zhang Guotao was sent after Zhou. When Zhang reached Nanchang, all the preparations were already in place, and besides, most of the representatives refused to take these orders. The 11th army and the 20th army under the command of He Long (1896–1969) had already come to Nanchang from Jiujiang city, and were welcomed by Zhu De (1886–1976), commander of the 9th army and head of the city police.

At two o'clock in the morning of August 1, 1927, the rebels began to attack the national Revolutionary Army guarding the city. After fighting for four hours, they occupied the city. But the Nationalist government gathered more troops to surround Nanchang. The rebellious army had to beat a retreat from the city and went south. On the way, Zhou Enlai, He Long and other leaders deserted their troops and escaped to Hong Kong and Shanghai. Only Zhu De led the rest of the army to Guangdong province. They had to adopt the stratagems of guerrilla warfare. In January of 1928, Zhu De started another riot and led his army to Mt. JingGang in Jiangxi province, where he met Mao Zedong. Their troops formed the Red 4th Army.

Mao Zedong resorts to rebellion

As Wang Jingwei expelled the members of the Communist Party from the Nationalist Party and the Wuhan government, Mao Zedong went to Changsha city on the 12th of August to arm peasants and mine workers in that area in preparation for a riot. He had an army of 8,000 soldiers. On the 9th of September, they started their rebellion and set out to attack Changsha city. There were many Communist Party members in the city, scheming to let the attackers in by making a sudden assault on the Nationalist government army guarding the city. But their plan was leaked by insiders and became known to the Nationalist government. The traitors had to escape or they would be arrested and killed. Mao had to change his plan of attack and marched towards Mt JingGang, where his forces united with Zhu De's army.

On the 4th of June in 1928, Zhang was forced to withdraw from Peking to go back to his original location. As he could not always accomplish what Japan demanded, Japan was not satisfied with him. On the fifth day, when Zhang was on board a train and passed through the railway station at Huanggutun, his train was exploded with gunpowder set there by the Japanese. He was severely injured and died when he reached Shenyang city. His son Zhang Xueliang (1901–2001) succeeded him in his position.

He declared he was joining the Revolutionary Army on 29th of December, 1928. There were no more warlords. China was thus united. It was not, however, at peace.

Chiang Kai-Shek Besieges the Red Army Five Times

The first siege

Since Chiang Kai-shek had cleared all the warlords from China, he began to deal with the Communist Party and the Red Army in October of 1930. Chiang sent his army, 300,000 strong, against the Red Army (the Chinese Workers and Peasants Red Army), 40,000 soldiers. If Chiang could surround the Red Army, he could easily wipe it out. But Mao's strategy was wiser than Chiang's. On November 1, Mao faked some maneuvers so that the Chinese Red Army seemed to be advancing in different directions, leading Chiang's commander-in-chief to think that the Red Army would escape. Therefore, the Nationalist Army split up in order to chase down the enemies in different directions. Then the Red Army gathered together again and annihilated a small national division of 9,000 soldiers that had been cut off from the main force on December 30, 1930. And the other divisions had to fall back. Thus ended the first siege.

The second siege

On the 1st of April, 1931, the second siege began. Considering the failure of the first siege due to the failed tactic of attempting to surround the Red Army, Chiang Kai-shek decided instead to move slowly with all the troops keeping close. On the 13th of May, the 28th division of the fifth army of the national forces left Futian and marched eastward. On the fifth day, Zhu De and Mao directed their 3rd military bloc and the 35th Red Army to form a left wing, and the 3rd Red Army to head up the middle, while the 4th Red Army and 12th Red Army made up the right wing, to surround the fifth Nationalist Army. The commander of this army committed the same mistake. He should not have marched separately from others. Zhu De and Mao ordered their 7th Red division and 35th Red division to block the advance of the reinforcements from the 19th Nationalist army. As a result, on the 16th day, the 28th division of the Nationalist Army was annihilated by the overwhelming number of enemy forces. On the 19th day, the 12th Red army attacked the 54th Nationalist division, which escaped. The 19th Nationalist Army had no information about what was happening to the other armies and had to retreat. Thus ended the second siege.

The third siege

On the 21ˢᵗ of June, 1931, after the two failed sieges, Chiang Kai-shek formed two military blocs 300,000 strong for the third siege. On the July 10, the Communist Party also made all possible preparations for battle. The Nationalist Army had started to march on July 1, but could not ascertain the location of the Red Army. Towards the end of the month, the main forces of the Red Army were found taking a back route to a place called XingGuo. From the enemy's location, Chiang Kai-shek judged that the Red Army planned to go west to cross the Gan River. He wanted to wipe it out on the east bank of the river. Mao and Zhu's original plan was to ignore the main forces of the Nationalist Army, and use the Red Army to break through the encirclement at Futian to assail the detachment remaining in the rear; but this plan was detected. The 11ᵗʰ and the 14ᵗʰ divisions of the Nationalist Army marched faster to occupy Futian to block the Red Army's escape route. This time, it looked good for Chiang. But Mao changed to a bold plan. He ordered the 35ᵗʰ Red Army to disguise itself as the main force, and to cross the Gan River to distract the Nationalist Army. On the 4ᵗʰ of August, his main forces stole between the gap between the two military blocs of the Nationalist Army before they closed like a vise. (That gap is said to have been 40 *li* wide. The *li*, or "Chinese mile," creates some difficulties as this traditional unit of distance was only recently standardized. It now means half a kilometer or about a third of a mile.) This strategy was successful and the Red Army arrived at a safe place and annihilated a brigade of the Nationalist Army there on August 7. Then the Red Army moved to Huangpo and wiped out four Nationalist regiments on the 11ᵗʰ.

Then Chiang Kai-shek found out that what he was pursuing was not the main force of the Red Army. When the Nationalist troops turned back to march north, the fatigued army was like an arrow at the end of its flight. On the 18ᵗʰ of September, the 9/18 event happened, so Chiang had to go back to Nanking to take charge of the situation. Thus ended the third siege.

The strategies Mao used in the previous three battles would be seen repeated and repeated. Chiang was defeated three times by the same stratagem. Chiang Kai-shek never learned from his failures and made little improvement. It could be said that he deserved to be driven away from the mainland to Taiwan, after all.

The establishment of the Red government in Ruijin

After a few victories, the Communist Party founded their Red government in Ruijin city of Jiangxi province. It was located in a basin with mountains on three sides. Nanchang city, the capital of the province, under the Nationalist government, was 300 li (just over 90 miles) away.

On the 7th of November, 1931, they celebrated the founding of the Red government. Mao was the Chairman of the government and Zhu De was the Commander of the army. In the area of the Red government, almost everyone was in an organization of some sort. The organization for six-year-olds and up was called the "children's league." That of the teenagers (fifteen-year-old and up) was called young pioneers. Young adults joined the "Red Guard Army." They printed their own paper money and used terrorist methods to control people. Even their own comrades were killed. Li Wenlin, also a leader in the party, was murdered. Peasants in that area did not have to give part of their harvest to any landowners, but they did have to support the Red government in order to support the Red Army.

No one could leave the area without a pass. There were sentinels everywhere, 24 hours a day. Whoever was caught leaving secretly would be executed. War time or not, under such drastic terrorism even the close subordinate Yang Yuebin deserted Mao and went to the Nationalist government to give away Mao's location. Airplanes were sent to bombard the place and Mao had to move.

The fourth siege

After the 9/18 and 12/8 events (detailed in Chapter 3) were over, with the signing of the Songhu armistice agreement in May of 1932, Chiang Kai-shek planned for the fourth siege. This time he attacked the district of Hubei, Hunan and Anhui provinces where the Red Army was weak and was soon vanquished. Then in February of 1933, Chiang concentrated his forces to push forwards to where the main forces of the Red Army camped. The leadership of the Red Army had been changed at the meeting in

Ningdu town in October of 1932. Mao Zedong was dismissed from the commanding position. The leader was Bogu, who came from Shanghai on the 7th of January, 1933, but the actual commanders of the Red Army were Zhu De, Zhou Enlai and Peng Dehuai (1898–1974).

They used the same ruse Mao had used. They ordered the 11th Red army to disguise themselves as the main forces to attract and lead off the middle, second and third columns of the Nationalist Army to Lichuan area, while their actual main forces rested at Guangchang. Then they laid ambushes for the 1st Red military bloc and 3rd Red military bloc and 21st Red army to attack the 52nd Nationalist Army, while the 5th Red military bloc and 22nd Red army would attack the 59th Nationalist Army. On March 1, both nationalist armies were annihilated and the commanders were captured. So the Nationalist Army was forced to withdraw. Thus ended the fourth siege.

The fifth siege

In May of 1933, Chiang Kai-shek set up his headquarters in Nanchang city and assumed the responsibility of commander-in-chief himself for the fifth siege of the Red Army. Since the last siege, the Red Army had grown considerably. Chiang Kai-shek therefore gathered an army a million strong, including the 300,000 of Chen Jitang's soldiers in Guangdong province. Chen had been a warlord there and had subordinated himself to the national government when he saw all the other warlords had been wiped out.

The siege began on September 25, 1933, and ended on October 14, 1934, lasting for 385 days. Chiang Kai-shek used artillery and airplanes. On the 25th day, the Nationalist Army attacked Lichuan town. After three days, they took the town. On the 9th of October, the 24th Red division went to attack Xiaoshi, but the Nationalist Army had a strong defense there with fortresses and trenches. For several days, the Red Army could not take the town, and suffered heavy casualties. That was the first stage.

In November, there was a coup d'état in Fujian province against Chiang Kai-shek. The leaders of this coup founded another government, but they had little support. Even the Communist Party declared this new government unlawful. So the coup ended in failure.

On the 11th of December, the Nationalist Army in town changed from defense to counterattack. The Red Army fought back under the command of the Central Committee of the Communist Party, regardless of the fact that the Nationalist Army was far better equipped. The Red Army was conquered and retreated. That was the second stage.

On April 10, 1934, Chiang Kai-shek sent 11 divisions divided into two columns marching towards Guangchang. The Communist Party used 9 divisions to prevent the Nationalist Army from attacking the town. Battles broke out in many other places, too. The Red Army lost in those places and had to withdraw to Guangchang. On the 27th of April, the Nationalist Army attacked the town and occupied it in the evening. The Red Army had to escape, leaving 5,500 casualties. That was the third stage.

In June of 1934, the Communist Party made up its mind to resist the Nationalist Army assault to the last man. Even so, on August 5, nine divisions of the Nationalist Army, with air support, defeated the Red Army. The remnants of the Red Army had to escape and began the famous Long March. That was the final stage of the fifth siege.

The Red Army failed because the commanders changed from the right strategy to a wrong one. During this period Mao Zedong was not in the Red Army. He had been sent somewhere else. The failure drove home the obvious point that strategy is more important than many other factors; strategy can be decisive; and especially in politics and war, strategy is everything.

The Famous Long March

The central Red Army, 86,000 in all, began marching on the 21st of October, 1934. This wound up being a 2,500-li march, that is, some 775 miles. They were headed to the western Hunan province where the 2nd and 6th Red military blocs encamped. Chiang Kai-shek deduced what route they were likely to take and laid four blockade lines to stop them. Zhou Enlai and Zhu De went to have a talk with Chen Jitang, a former warlord, and bribed him to let them go through his blockade line. So there was no fighting at the first three lines, as the Red Army never went there. However, they had to fight the Nationalist Army when they attempted to break through the fourth line. They made a heavy sacrifice after the rest of the Red Army fought through the fourth lines. Only 30,000 were left out of the 86,000.

The Long March could be divided in four stages. Firstly, the escaped Red Army wanted to go to a place at the border of Sichuan, Hunan and Guizhou provinces, where the geographic features were easy to defend and hard to attack. In these areas there were still some local small warlords that they could mingle amongst for safety and the central Nationalist government would not easily reach them. In early December, they climbed over some mountains and occupied Liping town in Guizhou province on the 14th of December, 1934.

Secondly, at a meeting in Liping on the 28th of December, Mao Zedong strongly opposed the plan to unite with the 2nd and 6th Red military blocs, and proposed to go to the border of Sichuan and Guizhou provinces to occupy the area round Zunyi town as a new military base. His proposition was accepted by the Central Committee, because from their present location, it was difficult to communicate with the two Red blocs. On the 7th of January, 1935, they took Zunyi town.

Here they held the famous Zunyi meeting, in which Mao was appointed to the command of the Red Army again.

Thirdly, though they wanted to establish a new military base in the vicinity of Zunyi town, the Nationalist Army continued to harass them. They had to escape to the northern Sichuan province, where Zhang Guotao, in command of the 4th Red military bloc, already set up a base. But that was far away, and they would have to cross various streams. From January to May of 1935, they ran here and there to avoid being destroyed by the Nationalist Army. They failed three times in crossing the Chishui Stream. Once they were forced to go back to Zunyi town. On the fourth try, they stole across the stream, then crossed Jinsha Stream and Dadu Stream. They met Zhang Guotao on the 16th of June. Then Mao suggested that they should march towards the northern Gansu province so that they might escape into the Soviet Union when necessary. But Zhang Guotao had three plans. The first plan was that they should go to create a base in northern Sichuan province, southern Gansu province and Xikang province. The second plan was that they should go to the northern Shaanxi province. The third plan was to go west into Xinjiang province.

Fourthly, the two blocs (the central Red Army, renamed as the 1st red military bloc) went together north from the 12th of June to the 7th of July. Then as both Mao and Zhang were in disagreement as to the future plan, each went his own way. Zhang, after marching through the grasslands, refused to keep going north but went back through the grasslands again to Xikang province and wanted to establish his base there. And Mao Zedong, together with Peng Dehuai, Lin Biao (1907–1971), and Ye Jianying (1897–1986), went to southwestern Gansu province. In October 1935, Mao and his men, only about 3,000 left, surmounted the Liupan Mountain and reached the northern part of Shaanxi province. To their surprise, Liu Zhidan was there with his 7,000 men. So they settled there.

As for Zhang Guotao, who had started with 80,000 men, he wanted to found a new Central Committee of the Communist Party and to be the chairman himself. But most of his men during through the Long March. He had no hope for his personal ambitions, so he turned himself in to the Nationalist Party. The Communist Party called him a traitor.

It happened like this: on April 4, 1938, leaders of both the Nationalist Party and the Communist Party were to go to worship at the mausoleum of Emperor Huang, a legendary hero recorded in Chinese history books, supposed to have lived five thousand years ago. Zhang went there as the chairman of the Communist Party and met Jiang Dingwen, a leader of the Nationalist Party. After the rites were concluded, Zhang told his attendants to go back first as he had something else to deal with. But he jumped into a car the Nationalist Party provided for him. And he was gone. He was no longer a member of the Communist Party. At the end of 1948, he arrived in Taiwan in poverty. He seemed to be a forgotten man. In the winter of 1949, he went to Hong Kong with his wife and three sons. In 1958, he went to Canada where his eldest son lived. In 1976 he had a stroke and was paralyzed on the right side. He died on December 2, 1979, at the age of 82.

An interesting note from recent times: People doubted the actual distance the Red Army covered. Therefore, on November

3, 2003, two young Englishmen started on their way to retrace the route the Red Army had covered. They spent 384 days and covered 13,000 li, not 25,000 li.

The military coup d'état in Xian City

As Japan invaded northeastern China (details in Chapter 3), the Communist Party seized this opportunity to demand that the Communist Party and the Nationalist Party unify against Japan in January, 1936. And as Japan occupied the northeastern China, Zhang Xueliang was driven out. Therefore, Chiang Kai-shek ordered Zhang to besiege the Communist Party in northern Shaanxi province on the 20th of September, 1935. But on the 1st of October, in the battle at Mt. Lao, the Red Army annihilated two regiments of Zhang's army. On the 29th, in another battle, the 107th division and the 619th regiment of Zhang's army were wiped out, too. On the 22nd of November, his 109th division went alone towards Wuqi town and camped on the way at Zhilu town for the night. The division commander thought that the Red Army was far away and could not attack him, so he let down his vigilance. However, the Red Army took a quick march all night long and surrounded the division. In the morning, the Red Army put the division to rout.

After these defeats, Zhang Xueliang made secret contact with the Communist Party seeking a truce. On the 9th of April, 1936, Zhang went to YanAn city to talk with Zhou Enlai, the representative of the Communist Party. Zhang Xueliang accepted the Communist Party's demand to unite against Japan. Zhang Xueliang even put in a request to join the Communist Party. Nevertheless, his request was not granted because his father, Zhang Zuolin, a warlord in the northeastern China, had killed some Communist Party members. Anyway, when Deng Xiaoping (1904–1997), an important leader of the Communist Party, was dangerously ill, Zhang procured medication for him and saved his life.

Chiang Kai-shek heard about the situation and was upset with Zhang Xueliang. But at the time, an event happened in Canton, on the 1st of June, 1936, called the 6/1 event. Chen Jitang in Guangdong province and Li Zongren (1891–1969) in Guangxi province wanted to be independent from the central national government, and on that day they sent a telegram from Canton to the central government asking permission to go north to fight Japan. But their real aim was to overthrow the central government.

Chiang Kai-shek sent his army to conquer Chen in Guangdong province and simultaneously brought over Chen's subordinates. In July, the commander of Chen's air force betrayed him and turned over to Chiang Kai-shek by flying 70 airplanes under his command to Nanking. Then the commander of his 1st army declared his loyalty to Chiang Kai-shek. So on the 18th of July, Chen Jitang escaped to Hong Kong. Then Li Zongren in Guangxi province had to announce his obedience to the central government.

On the 22nd of October, Chiang Kai-shek flew from Nanking to XiAn city to urge Zhang to continue the attack of the Red Army, but Zhang raised objections. They had a quarrel and Chiang went to Luoyang city. On the 29th day, Zhang went to Luoyang for the celebration of Chiang Kai-shek's birthday. He wanted to persuade Chiang to unite with the Communist Party against Japan, but Chiang refused. On the 27th of November, Zhang asked to go and fight Japan, but was rejected by Chiang. On the 2nd of December, Zhang flew to Luoyang to inform Chiang that his army might riot and asked Chiang to go to XiAn to talk to his soldiers. This was really a trick to lure Chiang there for a certain purpose. Chiang Kai-shek, unwise as ever, agreed and flew to XiAn with Zhang on the 4th of December. He lodged at Huaqing Pool on Lishan Mountain. Huaqing Pool was a resort built around a bathing pool with hot spring water. Actually the bathing pool was also inside a room. It was built in Tang Dynasty (AD 618–907) for the famous Yang, imperial concubine of Emperor Xuanzong (AD 685–762).

On December 9, the Communist Party organized a demonstration with crowds. A boy was said to be injured by the police, which incited the wrath of the mob. Zhang went to see Chiang Kai-shek, who wanted Zhang to stop the demonstration, but Zhang did not follow Chiang's instruction. On December 11, at night, Zhang summoned his generals and asked them to make preparations for a military coup the next day. Accordingly, in the morning of December 12, Zhang went to see Chiang Kai-shek with soldiers and took him into custody.

That evening, Mailing Soong, Chiang Kai-shek's wife, was told of the event and immediately thought of Donald William Henry (1875–1946, died in Shanghai), an Australian reporter, who was a friend of both Chiang and Zhang. Soong and Henry immediately took the train to Nanking. At 8 o'clock in the morning on December 13, Soong sent Zhang a telegram and Henry did, too, saying that they would be flying to XiAn city. On December 16, the Nationalist government ordered Zhang to release Chiang at once, but Zhang declined. So the government gathered, intending to attack XiAn, and prepared to send bombers. The Communist Party suggested killing Chiang. But on the 17th, Stalin wrote to the Communist Party saying that he was opposed to killing Chiang, who, in his opinion, would be a qualified leader in resisting Japan. He demanded that Chiang Kai-shek be released. So the Communist Party agreed.

When Soong and Henry arrived in XiAn, they went to see Chiang Kai-shek at once. Soong persuaded Chiang to go along with the plan, saying that it would be better to act against Japan than to be killed by the Communist Party. As a player in the anti-Japan resistance, he would be a hero. Killed by the Communist Party, he would be nothing. So Chiang Kai-shek accepted the agreement on the 24th day about the unity with the Communist Party to fight Japan, etc. But he did not sign on the agreement. Some of Zhang's subordinates were not satisfied. Zhang said that if Chiang wanted to go back from the agreement once he was released, he would do that even if he signed the agreement. If Chiang kept his promise, what did it matter that he signed it or not.

Chiang Kai-shek was let go in the afternoon of December 25, and Zhang accompanied him back to Nanking; he was kept in secret confinement till Chiang Kai-shek died on April 5, 1975. Then he was restored to freedom and died on October 15, 2001, in Hawaii. This event ended the war between the Communist Party and the Nationalist Party and began the Sino–Japanese war all over China.

Chiang Kai-shek

CHAPTER 3. THE JAPANESE INVASION OF CHINA

Events Leading Up to the Sino–Japanese War in 1937

The 9/18 event

The Japanese army had begun entering China even during the latter stages of the Qing Dynasty. Around the beginning of the 20th century, Russia had built a railroad in northeastern China. In 1905, Russia and Japan had had a war there, on the territory of China, and Japan took control of the part of the railroad from Changchun city south, called the South Manchuria Railway.

A legend about the origin of the Japanese says that 2,000 years ago, when the first emperor of the Qin Dynasty was on the throne, his next ambition was to live eternally. He sent a man by name of Xu Fu to go east in ships together with 100 boys and 100 girls. It was said that there were islands in the eastern seas on which dwelt immortals. The errand of Xu Fu was to find these immortals and ask for an elixir. Once he got it, he was to bring it back to the emperor. Xu Fu reached the Japanese islands and lived there with boys and girls, never returning to China. Those were said to be the earliest inhabitants and the earliest ancestors of the Japanese.

About 10:22PM on September 18, 1931, some Japanese soldiers laid gunpowder under the rails of the South Manchuria railway for blew it up. This part of the line went by the Liutiao Lake, a bit north of Shenyang city. Then they left three Chinese corpses in the uniform of Chinese soldiers as evidence that it was Chinese soldiers who had blown up the rails. On this excuse, the Japanese army attacked the Chinese army in Shenyang city. The Chinese army was ordered not to cause trouble with the Japanese army, so two of the three Chinese regiments guarding the city withdrew. But the third 620th regiment did not receive the order, and of course, resisted the attack. The next afternoon, Japanese reinforcements came and the Japanese army entered the city. They encountered resistance and fought street by street till all the regiment fled the city. This was called the Liutiao Lake Incident (or Mukden Incident, by foreigners), and was the beginning of the whole 9/18 event, although they had not yet declared war.

On September 19, Japanese army attacked and conquered 18 towns along the South Manchuria Railway. The defensive Chinese army in Changchun city also counterattacked the Japanese army, but on the next day, the city fell into Japanese hands. On September 21, Xie, chief-of-staff of the headquarters of the Chinese army in Jilin province, changed sides and went over to Japan. So the Japanese army took Jilin. On October 1, Zhang Haipeng, guarding Tiaoliao town, changed sides, and under instruction from the Japanese sent three regiments of his army to assault Qiqihar city, but on October 16 they were defeated by the Chinese defenders. By the 26th of October, the Japanese army had occupied the chief towns along the Sitiao Railroad. From November 4 to 18, the Chinese army in Heilongjiang province fought the Japanese army. Then they had to retreat from Qiqihar after leaving heavy casualties, and the next day, the Japanese army entered it.

At the start of the 9/18 event, Zhang Xueliang, who was responsible for all the northeastern provinces, left Shenyang for Jinzhou. On the 8th of October, the Japanese army sent 12 bombers to raid Jinzhou. On the 15th of December, after occupying the important towns of Heilongjiang province, the Japanese army began to attack Jinzhou. On the 17th, reinforcement came directly from Japan. On December 28, the 2nd division of the Japanese army crossed Liao River to attack Jinzhou. On January 3, 1932, the Japanese army took Jinzhou. On February 5, the Japanese army occupied Harbin city. These battles are still not written in Chinese history as indicating the outbreak of the Sino-Japanese War.

The army in the northeastern provinces under the command of Zhang Xueliang had 18 brigades of foot soldiers, five independent brigades of cavalry, and four regiments and a battalion of artillery, plus 262 airplanes and fleets. They could have fought off the Japanese invaders, but they simply abandoned the northeastern provinces. A shameful strategy.

The 1/28 event

After Japan occupied northeastern China, it took aim at southeastern China.

Shanghai was an ideal place for Japan. At 4 o'clock in the afternoon on January 18, 1932, five Japanese monks were instructed by the traitor Kawashima Yoshiko, formerly the Last Princess of Manchuria and now a Japanese spy using a Japanese name, to throw stones at workers at a Chinese factory. This caused a fight to break out. But some thugs were sent by the Japanese, and they beat one of the five monks to death and severely injured another. Then 50 Japanese young men went to the factory at midnight on January 19 and burned the factory down and murdered three policemen.

On January 20, around a thousand overseas Japanese in Shanghai held a demonstration to demand the Japanese consulate and the headquarters of the Japanese Marines take revenge on the Chinese. But on the way there, they began to riot and smashed Chinese shops.

On January 21, the Japanese general consul demanded the Mayor of Shanghai apologize, punish the murderers, make compensation for the losses, and disband all the anti-Japanese organizations. Although the mayor accepted all of these demands, the consul further ordered that the Chinese army back away from Zhabei district on the pretext that they posed a threat to the overseas Japanese. He added that if Chinese army did not leave before 6:00PM on January 28, they would attack. On January 24, more Japanese marines came to Shanghai. At 11:30 at night on January 28, Japanese marines attacked the Zhabei district in Shanghai, which was in the control of the 19th army of the Nationalist government. The 19th army fearlessly resisted the Japanese attack with the support of the people of Shanghai, which forced the Japanese to accept the mediation of England and America for a truce. But on February 3, the fight started anew. On the 23rd, a fierce battle took place and 3,000 Japanese marines and 2,000 Chinese soldiers were killed. On February 24, two more divisions from Japan arrived in Shanghai as reinforcements. Only the 5th army of the Nationalist government came to the aid. On March 3, with the mediation of England and America, the Songhu armistice was signed. The Chinese army were to be stationed in the region from Shanghai to Suzhou city. But Japan could still have their army in Shanghai.

One episode during all this took place on April 29 when Japan held a military parade in Hongkou Park to celebrate the birthday of the Japanese emperor, or "Sumera mikoto," and their victory. A Korean hero, disguised as a Japanese man, entered the park with a grenade in the shape of a water flask. When the Japanese were singing their anthem, he flung the grenade onto the platform, where it exploded. The chairman of the committee for the Japanese in Shanghai died on the spot. The commander of the Japanese army in Shanghai for the event was severely injured and died in the hospital. A regiment commander and the Japanese envoy for China each broke a leg. And one eye of the commander of the 3rd fleet was blinded. The Korean hero was caught and sentenced to death; he was sent to Japan and executed at a Japanese army base. After World War II, his remains were taken back to Korea and a monument was erected in his honor in Hongkou Park in Shanghai.

The establishment of Manchukuo

Afraid of international interference, Japan desired to establish a puppet government in northeastern China, and they thought of the abdicated emperor Henry. He was 18 years old when he was driven out of the Forbidden City on November 5, 1924; he escaped to the Japanese embassy and traveled to Tianjin city, and lived under the protection of Japan ever since. So he was their first choice for the puppet government.

Therefore, Henry was escorted from Tianjin city on the 10th of November, 1931, to Changchun city, where Manchukuo (meaning the state of Manchuria) was established on March 1, 1932, with Changchun as its capital and Henry as the head of Manchukuo.

Henry as head of Manchukuo

On the 15th of September, 1932, the Japan–Manchukuo Protocol was signed, in which Manchukuo asked that Japan station its army on its territory. On September 23, 1932, the Soviet Union consented to allow Manchukuo to set up consulates in Moscow and New Siberia. But the League of Nations reproved Japan for this and disavowed Manchukuo as an illegal entity. On February 24, 1933, the League of Nations declared that Manchuria belonged to the Republic of China, as the establishment of Manchukuo had not been decided by popular vote but by the government of Japan. The League of Nations adopted the "Stimson Doctrine" specifying that new states created by force of arms would not gain international recognition. Japan protested and withdrew from the League. of course, the Nationalist government in Nanking also refused to recognize it.

On March 1, 1934, the designation Manchukuo was changed to Manchu Empire, and Henry got to be Emperor once again. On May 24, 1934, El Salvador recognized the Manchu Empire. On April 6, 1935, Emperor Henry visited Tokyo, Japan, for the first time and the Sumera mikoto came to welcome him at the railway station. On November 28, 1936, Italy signed a protocol with Japan recognizing the Manchu Empire. On February 20, 1937, Germany recognized it and signed a treaty in Berlin on the 12th of May. In August of 1940, Denmark recognized the Manchu Empire. A handful of other nations also recognized it.

Flag of Manchu Empire

Changchun city, as the capital of this empire, had expanded to cover an area of 30 square miles by 1944 and its population reached 1,217,000, larger than the population of Tokyo at the time. The population was composed of Manchus, Han, Mongolians, Koreans, Russians, and of course, two million Japanese (as Japanese citizens, not subjects of the Manchu Empire). The total population was divided into different classes according to their different tribes. Among the regulations that reflected this stratification was one prohibiting non-Japanese residents from eating rice and white flour. Any non-Japanese resident, if found to have rice or white flour, was taken in as an "economical criminal." Three languages were used officially: Chinese (Han), Mandarin (the language of Manchu officials) and Japanese. As the population was mostly of the Han tribe, Chinese was the chief official language.

However, on February 24, 1942, Poland abolished its recognition of the so-called empire and in August, 1945, the empire came to an end when Japan surrendered and the Soviet Army occupied its territory. Henry abdicated once again on August 17 and was captured by the Soviet army as a prisoner of war.

He was handed over to the Communist Party of China. He was released on December 4, 1959, and died of uremia on October 17, 1967.

The 12/9 event

After Japan seized the northeastern provinces, they wanted to encroach more provinces further south such as Chahar and Hebei. They intended to establish another puppet government in these provinces. But the Chinese people had had enough. The students rose up in protest. At 10:00AM on December 9, 1935, three thousand students from universities and high schools in Peking demonstrated in opposition to such Japanese aggression. They fought with the police. Many students were injured and at least ten students were arrested. On December 10, all the students in Peking went on strike.

Students in Hangzhou followed suit. On December 11, the Peking government (still controlled by the Republic of China) sent policemen to the universities and schools to forbid the students going out to demonstrate. On December 12, students in Shanghai, Nanking, Wuhan, Canton, and many other big cities gave their support. The next day, the principals of six universities in Peking told the students that they must go back to classes since those who had been in custody were all released. On the 15th, the mayor of Peking invited student representatives to have a talk. On the 16th, the Peking government and the university authorities announced that any students who refused to attend class would be punished. But on the same day, 10,000 students went out to demonstrate again, and around 30 students were arrested and about 400 injured. Then 20,000 Peking residents joined in. Workers and shop owners all went on strike. On December 17, the mayor asserted that the students were being instigated by the Communist Party.

In January, 1936, students in Peking and Tianjin organized propaganda groups to go south among the workers and peasants to let them know about the invasion by Japan and calling on them to rise up against the Japanese. On March 31, Guo Qing, a student at the 17th high school in Peking, died in prison. Students indignantly crowded into the streets, carrying his coffin. On May 28, all Peking was protesting, with the slogans "Down with Japan" and "The 29th army must fight Japan." On May 30, the commander of the 29th army announced that if the Japanese army moved any further, it would face resistance. On June 13, students in Peking demonstrated again, and this time the police did not interfere; on the contrary, they showed their sympathy. On December 12, students held the fifth demonstration. These student protests, though not enough to prevent the Japanese from trespassing further into China, roused the Chinese people at large to resist the invaders.

The Outbreak of the Sino–Japanese War, Or the Anti-Japanese War

The double 7s event—Lugou Bridge event

At 7:30PM on the 7th of July (07/07), 1937, the Japanese army, stationed at the other side of Lugou Bridge over the Yongding River (with the Chinese army on this side of the bridge), 15 km from Peking, began to exercise, conducting a sham battle in the deserted fields under their control close to Wanping town. (Wanping had been founded in 1540 in the Ming Dynasty as a satellite town for the defense of Peking.) At about 12:40 that night, reports of gun shots were heard by the Chinese soldiers across the river. Japanese officers said that a soldier in their army had gone missing in the exercise and they heard reports of guns, so the soldier must have been killed by Chinese soldiers. On this pretext they tried to come into Wanping town to search for him. The Chinese army guarding the town, of course, refused their request, answering that everyone in the town was asleep and must not be disturbed, and besides, no Chinese soldier had fired a shot. Therefore, at 5 o'clock in the morning on July 8, they opened fire on the defensive Chinese army at this side of the bridge and also blasted the town with artillery. The Chinese army had to fight back. Historians consider this is the event that lit the fuse of the Sino–Japanese War.

Next day, the Communist Party sent out a public telegram to call on people to resist the Japanese invaders. And Chiang Kai-shek made a speech, saying, "No matter where you are, in the south or in the north, no matter who you are, old or young, everyone has the responsibility to resist, everyone must be determined to make a sacrifice." In the previous six years Chiang Kai-shek had stuck to a policy of not fighting the Japanese because he was not confident they could achieve the final victory, and he needed time to prepare. He had hired German advisors to train his officers and soldiers up to German standards. He stored ammunition and expanded his air force. He communicated with England, the US and Russia seeking diplomatic support. Though he lacked the self-confidence to win the war, he foresaw that the final victory belonged to China. As a small country, however strong militarily, Japan could never occupy such a big country like China.

In the first two days of fighting, Japan could see that they were not going to take the bridge easily. So they proposed peace talks to make time to gather more troops. Japan maneuvered its army from Korea and northeastern China to where the battles were, amassing 400,000 troops. On July 9, 11 and 19, peace agreements were signed three times, but they were useless, only serving to numb the Chinese army with a false outlook of peace.

On July 25, the Japanese army suddenly attacked the Chinese army stationed at Langfang, and 14 Japanese airplanes raided the barracks of the Chinese army. At noon on July 26, the Japanese army occupied Langfang. Then Japan demanded the Chinese army to withdraw from the region of Peking and Tianjin city, a demand that was of course rejected. At 1:00AM on July 26, a Japanese regiment started from Tianjin city and arrived at Fengtai, close to Peking, at 2:00PM. They asked to enter Peking to protect their citizens in the city. They were permitted in. When just half of the regiment was inside the city gates, the Chinese army fired at them. The regiment was cut in two, half inside and half outside the city. The inside half escaped to the embassy area, into the Japanese barracks in the Japanese embassy. The other half returned to Fengtai. On July 28, the Japanese army started to assault Peking. Chinese army resisted and suffered huge sacrifices. In the night of July 28, the Chinese army had to retreat from Peking. The next day, Japan took Peking, and the day after, Tianjin city fell into their hands as well.

The 8/13 event—battle in Shanghai

In southern China, Japan wanted to occupy Shanghai. On August 9, two Japanese marines in Shanghai drove a car and trespassed into the Hongqiao airport area to fire guns, but they were shot dead by the Chinese guards. On August 13, Japanese marines following their tanks attacked the Chinese army stationed along the Songhu railway, but they were beaten. On August 14, the Nationalist government made a statement calling for self-defense in resistance of Japan. The statement was really a general mobilization order to all Chinese people. The central national government organized several military blocs to defend Shanghai. On August 15, the Japanese government issued a statement, too, saying that in order to punish the Chinese army for its rash action and to urge the Nanking government not to take severe steps, the Japanese government had to resort to war. They sent more troops by sea to the Shanghai area. In joint action with the marines, the Japanese army planned to occupy the strategically important zone in the north of Shanghai.

Chiang Kai-shek divided the warring area into five zones. Shanghai was in the third zone. On August 17, the Chinese army counterattacked and the 87th division took the Japanese sailors' club. The 88th division fought Japanese troops in Hongkou park. The two divisions jointly broke through the Japanese defensive line to Huishan wharf. At the same time, the Chinese air force attacked that of Japan and also their warships. They downed 47 Japanese airplanes and sank one Japanese cruiser. Two divisions sailed from Japan to the eastern region of Shanghai, arriving on the 22nd. And on the 23rd, they landed at Wusong district. On August 24, the Chinese 15th military bloc entered Shanghai and assailed the two Japanese divisions just as they were setting foot on land. On September 1, a thousand Japanese soldiers attacked the Chinese cannon site and both had heavy casualties. Japan gathered 30 warships to support their army in an attack at Baoshan.

After September 11, Chiang Kai-shek himself took the command of the third zone. From then till the beginning of October, the Japanese army increased to 200,000 strong. But they did not have a decisive advantage over the Chinese army till early November. At dawn on November 5, under the cover of heavy fog and lifted by the rising tide, Japanese army landed at Hangzhou Bay. On November 6, they took Jinshan and used a vise strategy to attack the Chinese army from two sides. On November 8, under such unfavorable conditions, Chiang had to give order to retreat. On November 9, the Japanese army occupied Songjiang town and on November 12 they took Shanghai. During the battles, the people of Shanghai had contributed 3.3 million yuan to support the Chinese army.

The battles in Shanxi province

The Japanese army from the north marched toward Pingxing Pass in Shanxi province on the 24th of September, 1937, but the Chinese army was lying in wait for them. A Japanese regiment entered the ambush zone and was annihilated. On September 29, the Japanese army broke through the Chinese army's defensive line at Ruyuekou and attacked the rear of Chinese army at Pingxing Pass. The Chinese army had to beat a retreat to Taiyuan city, capital of Shanxi province. Qikou was an important strategic place, the gate to Taiyuan. On October 14, the Japanese army used a vise ruse to attack Qikou from two wings, but met with strong resistance. There were heavy casualties on both sides. On October 21, the Japanese army sent a division to attack Niangzi Pass with the intention of taking an indirect route to take Taiyuan from the north side. On October 26, a Japanese division sent a detachment to go round to the back of the Chinese army defending Niangzi Pass. The Chinese army in the Pass had to withdraw. The Japanese army took Niangzi Pass and chased the retreating Chinese to Yangquan. Then the Japanese army occupied Yangquan and marched toward Shouyang, closer to Taiyuan, on the 2nd of November.

Another Japanese military bloc took a different route and took Xiyang on its way to Taiyuan on November 2. The two Japanese blocs converged on Taiyuan. On November 3, the Japanese 5th bloc reached the northern edges of Taiyuan. On November 5, the Japanese broke through the Chinese defensive line and approached the city wall on November 6. In the meantime, the Japanese 20th military bloc penetrated the Chinese defensive line in the southern perimeter. On November 7, the Japanese army surrounded Taiyuan and on the 8th they began an onslaught on the city; at night they entered the city from the northern side. The Chinese army had to escape and then the Japanese army took the whole city.

In February of 1938, the Japanese 108th military bloc took Dongyang Pass and then another two towns. In early March, more towns were taken. By then all the important cities and towns in Shanxi province had fallen into the hands of Japan. Out of 105 cities and towns in Shanxi province, 102 of them were occupied by Japanese army.

The slaughter in Nanking

By October 1937, Nanking, the capital of the Nationalist government, was exposed to the attack of Japanese army. Therefore, Chiang Kai-shek decided to set up a temporary capital in Chongqing city in Sichuan province in southwestern China, at a safe distance from the Japanese army.

At first some generals persisted in defending Nanking at any cost. So the Nationalist government gathered 100,000 soldiers for that purpose. No matter, as Japanese army approached Nanking, the government at last had to declare that the government was moving to Chongqing city on the 20th of November. Government offices, universities and schools moved inland, one after another. Even residents of the city escaped from Nanking. In June, there were 1,015,000 residents in the city, but in December, only 468,000 or 568,000 remained. On the 20th of December, for humanitarian reasons, over 20 Westerners were still there organizing the international committee of the Nanjing safety zone to take in and protect refugees.

The Chinese national government recognized their efforts and supplied them with cash, food and police protection. Japan was far from pleased, but declared that if there were no Chinese soldiers hiding there, they would not attack it. But after they took the city, their soldiers forced entry into the zone, stealing private belongings, raping women and arresting and killing young men. Several times the international committee made protests to the Japanese embassy and Japanese army authorities, but in vain. During this slaughter, the committee protected 250,000 refugees. On the 18th of February, 1938, the organization was renamed the Nanking international rescue committee, acting only in a rescue role. By June, it was closed entirely.

On the 7th of November, Tokyo gave orders to limit the action of the Japanese army to the east of Suzhou and Jiaxing region. But the army ignored the order and pursued the retreating Chinese army, intending to occupy Nanking. They advanced quickly as no Chinese army fought them on the way. Seeing this, Tokyo issued orders to take Nanking on December 1.

The Japanese army marched so fast that their supply units were left far behind. When they were approaching Nanking, food was scarce. The soldiers pillaged the Chinese villages for anything edible and wantonly violated women. To cover their crimes, they even slew all the people in the village and burned everything. As they came to Nanking, at least 30,000 Chinese people were killed along the way. It was a rehearsal for the slaughter in Nanking.

On December 8, the Japanese army took all the defensive sites outside Nanking. The worst battle took place at Yuhua Terrace outside the city. Two Chinese brigades were guarding the place. From December 9–11, the Japanese army kept on sending reinforcements for the attack, aided by their artillery and air raids, until every Chinese soldier was killed. When the Japanese troops reached the terrace, no one was alive. Then the Japanese army cleared all the defensive lines outside the city, and the Chinese army in the city had to retreat. On December 13, the Japanese army entered the city. Some Chinese soldiers who did not have time to escape stripped off their uniforms and disguised themselves as civilians. Some ten thousand Chinese were taken captive. They were all killed on instructions from the Japanese army authorities. They also searched for other Chinese soldiers in disguise. Anyone they suspected was killed. Many of them were really unarmed civilians. They even murdered old people and children. They killed all the women they had raped.

On December 13, 1937, a Japanese newspaper, Tokyo nichi nichi (mainichi shimbun), reported that two Japanese officers, Mukai Ming and Noda Takeshi, had a competition to see who could kill more Chinese people. Encouraged by their superiors, they declared that whoever was first to kill 100 Chinese people was a hero. They practiced this slaying from Gourong to Tangshan, and Mukai Ming killed 89 while Noda Takeshi killed 78. Certainly, we can all agree they were not heroes. However, the competition continued. When they met at Mt. Zinjin, both had dented the blades of their swords. Noda Takeshi said that he had killed 105 and Mukai Ming said that he had killed 106. However, there was no witness. So they started the competition anew, aiming at 150. The newspaper ran pictures with captions. Both these brave men were executed in Nanking for their crimes after the surrender of Japan.

Statistics show that during the two months the Japanese occupied Nanking, about 80,000 women were raped, some of them pregnant, from girls as young as 12 to women as old as 65. Many died after the violence. They raped women right in front of their families. Many people were buried alive. The victims were forced by the Japanese soldiers to dig their own pits. During the six weeks of the occupation, 23.8% of structures inside and outside the city were destroyed by fire, 63% had been plundered and 88.5% were structurally damaged. They used military trucks to carry away their loot. By some estimates, 26,584 antique curios or artifacts were missing, such as bronze wares from the Shang Dynasty (1765–1122 BC), along with 7,720 paintings and 45,979 valuable books. Some 109,000 casualties were found and buried. The Nanking branch of the World Red Swastika Society gave out statistics in 1945 claiming that from December 22, 1937 to October 30, 1938, they found and buried 43,123 bodies—1,793 inside the city and 41,330 outside the city, including 75 women and 20 children. Those statistics were from just one organization. The victims totaled 300,000 in all.

Japanese slaughter in Nanking

The battles in Shandong province

Now the Japanese army occupied the north of China and also Shanghai and the Nanking area. What more could they want? Well, the Shandong province, which is between the northern provinces and the southern area. Shandong province was then still under the control of the Chinese army. Xuzhou city was a place of strategic importance. So battles were waged in its vicinity and expanding into adjoining provinces. If the Japanese army occupied Xuzhou, they could go west along the Longhai railway to attack Zhengzhou in Henan province and then go south along the Pinghan railway to attack Wuhan in Hubei province. So the Japanese army came down from the north and came up from the south.

At the beginning of the Anti-Japanese War in 1937, Han Fuju, the chairman of the government of Shandong province, was ordered to take charge of the defensive line along the Yellow River and prevent the Japanese army from crossing the river. But when the Japanese army rushed down upon him from the north, he fled as if to open the gate and invite the enemy in. The Japanese army easily crossed the river. In early March 1938, they occupied JiNan, the capital of Shandong province.

On the 26th of January, 1938, the 13th division of the Japanese army marched from the south towards Fengyang and Bangbu in Anhui province. The Chinese army stationed there, after efforts at resistance, fell back towards the west. On the 3rd of February, the Japanese division took Linhuai Pass and Bangbu. On February 9–10, the 13th division crossed the Huai River to the north. The 51st Chinese army stationed itself on the north bank and fought the Japanese army.

Between March 1–17, the Japanese army attacked Teng Town in the southern Shandong province. On March 14, the battle reached its climax. The Japanese army used 30 cannons. On March 17, Teng Town was lost.

Meanwhile in late February, the Japanese 5th military bloc came down to the south, after taking over a few towns, and approached Linqi Town where the 40th army of the Nationalist government held the defense. Then the 59th Chinese army came for reinforcement. From February 14 to 18, the 59th Chinese army attacked the Japanese bloc from the rear and one wing. The Japanese had to retreat this time, leaving behind heavy casualties.

On March 20 a Japanese brigade, after taking a few towns, approached TaiEr village area, which was the front defensive line to Xuzhou. The brigade attacked alone without waiting for the 5th division and another brigade of their army; they were supposed to break through the defensive lines on the left wing and on the right wing. From March 24, the Japanese army assailed fiercely. The 2nd Chinese military bloc held the line. Then the 20th Chinese bloc attacked the Japanese army from behind. The 59th Chinese army arrived in time to contribute their efforts. They surrounded the Japanese army. The 10th Japanese corps was wiped out and the 5th Japanese corps was put to rout. It was the first and only time that the Chinese army defeated the Japanese army in the early period of Anti-Japanese War.

Anyway, Japan aimed at taking Xuzhou. On the 18th of April, two Japanese divisions attacked the 20th, the 3rd and the 59th Chinese armies. On the 5th of May, the main forces of the Japanese army divided into two detachments and went from west side of Xuzhou to the north and south sides of the city, intending to surround it. On May 14, the 14th Japanese division came from Puyang in Henan province, and crossing the Yellow River, occupied Heze. On May 15, the Japanese army surrounded Xuzhou. So under the command of Chiang Kai-shek, the Chinese army in Xuzhou broke through the circle and escaped to the mountainous area in Henan and Anhui provinces. Xuzhou was at length taken by the Japanese army on May 19.

Now the Japanese army marched west along the Longhai railway and on the 6th of June occupied Kaifeng city in Henan province. To prevent the Japanese army from any further advance, Chiang ordered his men to blow up the south dike of the Yellow River at Huayuankou on May 9, on the northeastern side of Zhengzhou in Henan province. The water from the river flooded south and the Japanese army had to flee eastward. Thus ended the battles in Shandong province. Han Fuju was executed for running away from the battlefield and allowing the Japanese to cross the Yellow River unopposed.

The battles at Wuhan city area

After taking Nanking, the Japanese army wanted to conquer China in three months with blitzkrieg attacks like Hitler did in Europe. They marched along the Yangtze River towards Wuhan, gathering large numbers of troops, amounting to 300,000 strong. If they took Wuhan, half of China would be in their possession. But they neglected to consider that even so, they only occupied the cities and towns in this half of China, not the whole area. They had no manpower to control the countryside. As they pushed forward, they had to leave some of their troops to guard the cities and towns they had captured. And so they could use less and less troops, and then there were those lost in battle. Poor strategy.

The Chinese army totaled 1,100,000 in defense. The whole defensive line extended for 250 miles. The fighting went on for four and a half months, the longest in terms of time and the largest in scale of all the battles between Japan and China. The Japanese casualties were 35,500 while those of the Chinese army were 256,000. After that, the Japanese did not have enough forces in China to make the lightning attacks they preferred; now they had to change their strategy and concentrate on keeping a hold on what they had secured so far.

On the night of the 11th of June, 1938, a Japanese brigade, under the cover of a rainy night, gave a surprise attack and took Anqin the following day. Anqin was the first defensive spot en route to Wuhan. Then they went west by water, riding their warships. In late June, they arrived at Madang, where the Chinese army had built a strong defensive line. Chiang Kai-shek hoped that this line could block their advance for at least one month.

At first, the Japanese army wanted to get through the line by water. On June 22, they approached Madang and found that the water was full up mines, sunken ships, and artificial reefs so that their warships could not go through. They had to advance by land and break through the line through the mountainous areas.

Li Yunheng, the Chinese commander in charge of the defense in Madang, wished to show that he was a clever general— without realizing how serious the situation was. He organized a training class for officers in charge of regiments, battalions, companies and platoons in his army for two weeks starting on June 10. And at 8 o'clock in the morning June 24, he thought he would hold a ceremony marking the completion of the class. So on the 23rd, all the officers went to the headquarters and stayed there for the ceremony next morning. Someone in the training class was spying for the Japanese and gave this information to the Japanese army. So they sent surprise squads to attack some of the fortresses along the front. As there were no officers to direct the action of the soldiers, there was chaos and the squads took the fortresses easily. But when the squads went on to attack Changshan, they encountered strong resistance, because the officers there had refused to attend the ceremony. The fight lasted for two days and the Chinese troops were short of ammunition and telegrammed headquarters. The 167th division was sent as reinforcement. But Xue Weiying, the commander of this division, was a coward and approached slowly to avoid being killed in the battle. At dawn on the 26th, the Japanese squads stole through a thick patch of reeds to attack another frontier post. They used poisonous gas and killed all the defensive soldiers there. Then the Japanese army cleared all mines in the water by firing at them and got rid of other barriers. They shipped marines to attack Changshan and broke through the defensive line there. The Chinese defense had to withdraw out of Madang and the Japanese army occupied it. Madang was the 'gate' in the middle of the Yangtze River to Wuhan. Commander Li Yunheng was severely punished and the division leader Xue Weiying was executed for neglect of his duties.

After taking Madang, the Japanese army continued west. On the 29th of June, they took Pengze. Under orders from Wuhan headquarters, the 64th Chinese army came in hopes of taking back the town, but it was defeated and chased to Hukou, which was soon taken by the Japanese army on the 4th of July. The 64th Chinese army then went to Jiujiang, which was situated by the Poyang Lake. On July 22, the Japanese army attacked the city. At dawn on July 23, the Japanese army stole into the lake in the rain and set foot on the shore at noon. The Chinese defensive army did not see them coming. They spotted the enemy and reported to headquarters only at 4 o'clock. By then, the Japanese army had surrounded the city. The Chinese army inside had to fight through the circle and escape. The city fell into the hands of the Japanese army on July 24.

The next goal of the Japanese army was Tianjia town. The hilly ground was easy to defend and hard to attack. The river was only 500 meters wide. The Chinese army set up a strong defense here with artillery. On the 21st of August, the Japanese army attacked Matou town, about 10 miles downstream from Tianjia town, and took it after more than 20 days of struggle. On the 26th, the Japanese army sailed in warships upstream towards the town. There were more barriers in the water, so the Japanese army advanced very slowly. On August 29, another Japanese detachment went to attack Guangji. If they could take this town, they could go on to attack Tainjia from behind. Tianjia town was about 25 miles northeast of Guangji Town. The attack began on August 30 and lasted until September 6. Between Guangji town and Tianjia town there was only a narrow road between two small lakes. The Japanese army followed that road on September 15. There were some defensive outposts set along this road. Coming to a roadblock, they used poisonous gas again. Some Chinese soldiers were injured and the Chinese army had to retreat.

The Japanese marines went to Wuxue, some distance from Tianjia. Wuxue was defended only by a company of Chinese soldiers. In the evening of September 15, the marines began the offensive. The defensive soldiers fought the invaders alley by alley till only a few soldiers left, and they slipped away. But before they left, they destroyed the dike at the river bank and the water flooded Wuxue area, which hindered the advance of the marines.

A Japanese brigade that was surrounded by the Chinese army was running short of rations and ammunition. A Japanese commander learned about this and called for an air lift to re-supply them. So Japanese airplanes dropped the necessities and ammunition to the brigade. But as the fighting continued, their ammunition was soon used up. The Japanese soldiers were reduced to throwing stones at the Chinese attackers and sometimes threw back the grenades the Chinese soldiers cast at them. The Chinese army figured out that the enemy was in a tight spot and marched forth in a downpour of rain to wipe them out. However, more Japanese troops came to the rescue and assailed the Chinese army from behind, so they had to withdraw. Few men in the Japanese brigade were left alive.

On September 23, some of the wounded Japanese soldiers were shipped away, but the first field hospital was still full. Because of the lack of helping hands, those who were lightly wounded and who could still walk, went to the field hospital by themselves. Sometimes they had to crawl in the rain and in the mud. By the time they reached the hospital, they were almost dying. Some died on the way owing to the loss of blood. The hospital had little food to spare and could only give them what they had. War is cruel to all participants.

After the sunset on the 26th, the 4th Japanese battalion attacked Xinwo. Their soldiers all put on gas masks and cleared out the Chinese company there, except about ten of them who had already escaped. The Japanese soldiers then went in and used bayonets to kill any Chinese soldiers that had not died yet.

The 4th battalion went towards Lujia Mountain without leaving any soldiers to guard Xinwo. It was dark and the mountain contours were complicated. The 4th battalion lost its way in the mountains. The 339th Chinese regiment was taking shelter on this mountain. But after a few battles, only one battalion was left. As Xinwo was lost, the regiment commander chose some hundred soldiers to form an expendable squad to make one last try at Xinwo. When they reached there, they found no Japanese soldiers guarding the place. But by coincidence the 2nd Japanese battalion came into their firing zone. The Japanese troops thought that their 4th battalion had already wiped out the Chinese soldiers defending the city, but now they encountered the Chinese squad by surprise. So 61 soldiers of the 2nd Japanese battalion were killed and 17 escaped. At daybreak, the 4th battalion found that they were at the foot of Lujia Mountain and they climbed up to attack the Chinese soldiers on the top, who were just ready for breakfast. When they detected Japanese soldiers creeping up the mountainside, they disappeared.

In the early morning of September 28, the cannons from the warships on the river and from land poured heavy fire upon Tianjia and all the defensive structures and weaponry were destroyed. It looked like a sea of flames. At the same time, all the outer defensive spots were lost. The Chinese army in Tianjia was ordered to withdraw. At 10 o'clock on September 29, when the Japanese army entered the town, the Chinese defenders were nowhere to be seen.

At the same time, the 106th Japanese military bloc had been marching south along Nanxun railroad to Nanchang. On the August 20, this bloc, aided by the 101th Japanese bloc, broke through the Chinese defensive line at Xingzi. But the Chinese army had a second defensive line. The two Japanese blocs could not go further this time. In September 1938, a Japanese reconnaissance airplane found that there was a gap in the defensive line after the fight had been going on for a month. So the 106th Japanese bloc was sent to go stealthily through that gap and come upon the Chinese defensive army to attack them from behind. On September 25, the 106th bloc began to steal through the gap, but lost their way in the mountains. They were soon discovered and surrounded by Chinese soldiers. On October 7, the Chinese army attacked and the fight went on for three days. The bloc had no reinforcements and ran out of ammunition. On September 10, 3,000 Japanese soldiers died. The rest of escaped.

On the August 27, the 2nd Japanese army attacked Dabie Mountain area and took LiuAn and Huoshan. They split into two detachments. The first went through the Dabie Mountain area to approach Wuhan directly. The second detachment went to Lushan through a circuitous route to Wuhan. But Mt. Fujin was right on their way to Wuhan. They had to occupy Mt. Fujin first. A severe battle commenced. They failed to take the mountain by September 6. On September 11, the 16th Japanese bloc came for reinforcement. The Chinese defensive army in the mountains had to withdraw. As the Japanese army approached Wuhan, there was no more Chinese army seen. The Chinese army already retreated from Wuhan, leaving the city to the Japanese army.

Although the Japanese army took control of many cities and towns, they really did not annihilate the Chinese army, which still had enough strength to fight back when needed. On the contrary, the Japanese army suffered great losses and had no more strength to wage battles on a large scale. As China is such a huge country, even with all the Japanese armies thrown into the territory of China, they could not cover the whole area of the nation. Besides, when they took a city, they took on an additional burden. As they acquired more and more burdens, they had less and less strength to fight. That has to be factored into any military strategy.

The Japanese army takes Canton in the south

The top brass of the Japanese army had a meeting on September 7 and decided to overrun southern China as they had already occupied the northern and middle China. Their final goal was to occupy the whole of China and then occupy all the countries in East Asia to establish what they called Great East Asia Coprosperity Sphere.

However, historians question why they attacked Pearl Harbor, since Hawaii was not in East Asia. This ill-advised action, or ill-advised stratagem, made them pay heavily when America declared war against them. of course, even if they hadn't attacked Pearl Harbor, the United States would finally have joined the war in East Asia after Germany was conquered, because Japan was one of the axis countries, just as the Soviet Union entered northeastern China to fight the Japanese army.

Anyway, Chiang Kai-shek misjudged the situation, thinking that since Japan was still fighting in the Yangtze River area, they could not go south to Canton. So he maneuvered four divisions from the Canton area to support those battling in Wuhan. In other words, he weakened the defensive forces in Canton. But Canton was a harbor city, an outlet to the sea, a place of strategic importance.

On October 12, 1938, the Japanese 18th and 104th blocs set out for Canton by sea and air from the Pescadores Islands (located between the mainland and Taiwan, which was known at the time by the name Formosa, given by the Portuguese) with the aid of four aircraft carriers. They entered Daya Bay in the Guangdong province. The next day, they dropped bombs on Huiyang town and after three days, they took it. On October 19, they suddenly attacked Zengcheng and put the Chinese defenders to rout. On October 21, the Chinese army withdrew from Canton and the Japanese army took it. Another burden. On October 22, 110 Japanese airplanes and the 5th fleet pounced upon Humen, a very important strategic spot. Within ten days, they occupied Canton and Human.

The Japanese army attacks Changsha City three times

Although the Japanese army occupied Nanking and Wuhan, two big, important cities, there were other important cities in between that had not taken yet. Changsha was one of them. On the 14th of September, 1939, they gathered 100,000 soldiers and marched towards Changsha. But they had to fight through one Chinese defensive line after another.

The 101th Japanese bloc attacked GaoAn on September 18. On the 19th, the Chinese gave up the town after a severe fight and receded to Shiguling. Then, the Chinese 32nd army counterattacked in GaoAn on September 21. On September 22, the Chinese army took back GaoAn. The Japanese 106th bloc took Ganfang on September 24. The next day, the Chinese counterattacked in Ganfang. On the 6th of October, two Chinese blocs surrounded the Japanese army, who fled back to where they had come from. The Chinese army chased them and took back a few towns that had been captured by the Japanese army. On October 13, Chinese army stopped its pursuit. Thus ended the Changhsha battle for the first time, and the people there had a moment to recover.

In early September of 1941, Japan gathered 120,000 men, with artillery and air support, and marched on Changhai once more. On September 7, the Japanese 6th bloc attacked Dayun Mountain as a decoy to screen the gathering of their 3rd, 4th, and 40th blocs on the right bank of the Xinqiang River. The 4th Chinese army gave up the front line on the mountain. On September 10, the Chinese 58th army came as reinforcements and took back the mountain position. At the daybreak on September 18, the Japanese 3rd, 6th, and 40th blocs crossed the Xinqiang River and the next day they reached the north bank of the Miluo River. The Chinese 37th and 99th armies were stationed on the south bank of the river and they prevented the Japanese army from crossing. Meantime, the Chinese 20th, 58th, and 4th armies went to attack the Japanese army wing. But a telegram from headquarters to the armies at the front was intercepted and deciphered by the Japanese, who changed their plan and went to assail the Chinese army coming from their side. On September 24, the Japanese army crossed the Miluo River. On the 26th, the Japanese 4th bloc crossed Laodao river and the next day crossed Liuyang River and approached Changsha. On the afternoon of September 27, they entered the city from the southeast side and shortly occupied the whole city.

But Chinese armies came from all sides and surrounded the city. The Japanese supply lines were cut and provisions inside the city ran short. On October 1, they had to escape north. So the Chinese army pursued them. On October 5, they caught up with the runaways on the south side of the Miluo River and fought there. The Japanese army had to cross the river to the north side. On October 6, the Chinese army crossed the river, too, keeping up the chase, and they crossed the Xinqiang River on October 8. On October 11, the Chinese army restored all the positions taken by the foe. The second battle for Changsha was over.

After the 7th of December, 1941, when Japan made their semi-secret bombardment of Pearl Harbor, Japan was scheming to attack the Chinese army in Changsha area again lest they should go south to assist the Britain in the defense of Hong Kong.

On December 23, the Japanese army crossed the Xinqiang River once again to pounce upon the Chinese army in Changsha, who put up a firm resistance. Other Chinese armies around the area came to surround the Japanese army, who gradually ran low on ammunition and their supply line was cut off. On January 15, 1942, the Japanese army had to break through the encirclement and escape. They lost 50,000 soldiers.

The victory in these battles made a deep international impression just when the situation appeared unfavorable to the Allies in East Asia. On January 1, 1942, twenty-six nations held an assembly in Washington D.C., and made a joint declaration. The United States, Great Britain, the Soviet Union, and China, the four greatest powers in the world, signed the declaration. And Xue Yue, the commander of the Chinese army in the Changsha defensive war, was conferred a Medal of Honor by American government.

The battles in Nanning City

On the 1st of September, 1939, Germany invaded Poland. World War II broke out in Europe. Japan thought that it would be best to speed up the process of conquering China. Considering that China got all its supplies from international support through its southwestern border, Japan understood it had to cut off this supply line and China would soon surrender. Japan sent army and navy forces to occupy Nanning city in Guangxi province and took control of the railroads there. And the Chinese defensive forces were not so strong there as around Changsha.

On the 9th of November, 1939, the Japanese attackers gathered at Shanya Bay, ready for action. On the 13th, a Japanese fleet started out from Shanya Bay and arrived at Beihai on the 14th. As the Chinese army there was not ready to fight, Beihai soon fell to Japan. On November 17, the Japanese army took Qinzhou and continued north. Guided by bandits through the mountains in that area, the Japanese army accelerated its advance. On November 22, they reached the south bank of the Yong River in the vicinity of Nanning city. But at the time, Chinese armies had already arrived in the city and its outskirts.

On November 23, the Japanese army crossed the Yong River with air cover. At dawn on November 24, the attack on the city began. The Japanese army saw strong resistance, but took the city at last in the afternoon. The Chinese army retreated to Gaofeng Pass. On November 26, the Japanese army attacked the pass, and they captured it by December 1. Three days later they had Kunlun Pass as well. Then, both sides held their respective positions for a while. No fighting went on.

On December 7, the Chinese army began to attack the invaders. On December 16, the Chinese army surrounded Kunlun Pass. The newly organized Chinese 22nd division went round the pass from its right side to block Japanese reinforcements from Nanning. Two regiments went round from its left side to block the Japanese army's escape route. At daybreak on December 18, the Chinese army commenced the assault and took Kunlun Pass. At the noon the next day, the Japanese army came back and took the Pass again. It changed hands several times. On December 18th, the Chinese 170th division attacked the Gaofeng Pass defended by the Japanese army and took a hilltop nearby, but that same night, the Japanese army gave a surprise attack and occupied the hilltop again. On December 20, the Japanese army at Kunlun Pass could not hold out anymore. And the reinforcements were blocked. In the afternoon of December 26, both Japanese forces escaped and safely arrived in Nanning.

At night on December 28, the Chinese army attacked Jieshou Highland, the gate to the Kunlun Pass. The following morning, the Chinese army took the highlands, and on the 30th of December, the Chinese army took Kunlun Pass. On December 31, they wiped out all enemies in the area of Kunlun Pass. If the Chinese army could have advanced in the pursuit of their enemies at the time, the situation might have been different.

On January 1, 1940, Japan sent reinforcements, and the warfare continued. On the 7th, Chiang Kai-shek flew to Huilin city and on January 10, went to the headquarters at Qian River to hold a meeting with all the frontier commanders. At that time, Japan had not gathered all the forces it needed. So at the request of some of the commanders, Chiang decided to launch an attack, but next day, when he returned to Liuzhou, he changed his mind and missed the chance to annihilate the remaining foe in that area.

On January 14, 3,000 Japanese soldiers landed in Qinzhou, and two days later, they began to assail the Chinese army. On the 27th, the Japanese army resumed their assault. The Chinese commanders did not have enough information about the maneuvers of the Japanese army and made a terrible mistake. They did not have enough time to make proper arrangements.

On February 1, the Japanese army made their all-out attack. But Chiang changed the commander-in-chief at the front, which really runs counter to the fundamental rules of the art of war. In the afternoon on February 2, the Japanese army entered Binyang town. On February 3, they took Kunlun Pass and other spots. The Battles for Nanning city ended in failure for the Chinese.

It was actually Chiang Kai-shek's fault, as he often changed orders, confusing his subordinates. Chiang Kai-shek was not really a good commander himself, though he had graduated from a famous military academy in Japan. He should have been able to beat Mao, who had no such advantage but only learned his tactics from Chinese history books. This leads to the inevitable conclusion that Mao was more intelligent than Chiang Kai-shek. Every Chinese person knows that Chiang Kai-shek's rulership was bad, but many found that the rule of the Communist Party under Mao was worse. Part of this is due to personal character-istics of the leaders, part of it is due to the fact that under Mao China remained on a more-or-less war footing under constant menace from the West, and some of it depends on the position of the people talking. Obviously, when the Communists started expropriating private property, those who had something to lose were never going to forgive them. Some historians said that if Chiang could have beaten Mao, the Chinese people wouldn't have suffered so much during all the cruel political movements under Mao, some of which were quite poorly thought-out and highly destructive. Even so, no one can claim that the regime in Taiwan, after Chiang Kai-shek's eventual defeat, was either democratic or open.

The battles of 100 regiments of the Communist Party

In the Anti-Japanese War, most battles were waged between the Japanese army and the army of the Nationalist government. The Communist Party, though having their own army, did their best to shun any major fights with Japan so that they would still have enough forces to fight Chiang Kai-shek after the Anti-Japanese War; this way, they could seize power and rule China.

That was why Mao Zedong thanked the first Japanese del-egation when they came to China for saving the Communist Party, and himself too, from the destruction Chiang might have inflicted on them, if Japan hadn't invaded China. Mao graciously gave up the right to war indemnities from Japan, regardless of the demands of the Chinese people for some compensation for their extraordinary losses.

Anyway, at that time, Japan also wanted to occupy the terri-tory the Communist Party possessed. So warfare did break out at last between the Japanese army and the army of the Communist Party, from the 20th of August to the 10th of September, 1940, in the first stage. The Japanese army was 300,000 strong, while the Communist Party had gathered 105 regiments. They called this the "100 regiments battles." Their commander-in-chief was Peng Dehuai. At that time, the Red Army changed their name to the 8th Route army, included in the military system of the National-ist government. Their aim was to damage the railroads so that the Japanese army could not get supplies by train. They attacked

Zhengtai railway, Tongpu railway, Pinghan railway, and Jinpu railway, especially Zhengtai railway, the main route for the traffic of the Japanese army. Japan in the northern China didn't have so many soldiers to guard every inch of the rails and as a result, all the four railways did not function any more after the attacks.

From the 22nd of September to the 10th of October, for the second stage, the 8th Route Army attacked some important strategic spots controlled by Japan. At 8:00PM that day, the 8th Route Army began to attack the Lailing area and took some Japanese front fortresses round Laiyuan town, but they could not break through the defense of the town itself because they did not have effective weapons for that kind of attack. On September 23, they stopped besieging the town and changed their stratagem to first seize the defensive spots outside the town.

On September 25, they turned to attack the stronghold at Dongyuan. The Japanese army inside gave a robust resistance, even using poison gas. However, they were forced to withdraw to the central redout, which the 8th Route Army then surrounded. As the Japanese soldiers knew that they could never escape, they committed suicide by self immolating.

On September 28, 3,000 Japanese soldiers came as reinforcements. That changed the situation and it was no longer possible to attack the town and so the Chinese forces withdrew. On October 1, the Japanese army took back most of the places that the 8th Route Army had occupied. On October 7, the Japanese army at Lingqiu got some intelligence indicating that the 8th Route Army was planning to attack their position, and so the Japanese just headed out to meet the right wing detachment of the 8th Route Army and give them a trouncing. From the night of October 8 to dawn, the left wing detachment of the 8th Route Army took their chances now that the Japanese army had left their position; they took it over as well as other positions in the vicinity. But on October 10, the 8th Route Army learned that the Japanese army had gathered together and would clean out the area where the 8th Route Army was in place, so they withdrew from the combat. Thus ended another 18 days of warfare.

In this period, the 8th Route Army had suffered heavy casualties, more than the Japanese army had lost. After the combat, Mao Zedong criticized Peng Dehuai for losing so many soldiers.

Mao's intention was to keep his losses as low as possible so that he could fight Chiang Kai-shek after the Anti-Japanese War. But during the Japanese army's clean-up operation, the 8th Route Army always retreated to elude any fight with the Japanese army. They called this the mobile warfare strategy. So the Japanese army just vented their disappointment and wrath on the common Chinese people who had supported the 8th Route Army. Records show that on the 25th of January, 1941, when the Japanese army ran a clean-up operation without finding any 8th Route Army soldiers in the northern Hebei province, they just encircled a village called Panjiayu in the area of Fengrun town and slaughtered 1,237 villagers and burned 1,000 houses there. The 8th Route Army had already escaped, deserting the villagers.

The campaigns in northern Burma and western Yunnan province

In 1942, a detachment of the Chinese Nationalist government army went to Burma through Yunnan province to help fight the Japanese army, who had entered Burma through Thailand on the 4th of January, 1942, and occupied Rangoon (Yongon) on the 8th of March. Japan's goal was first to cut off the supply line to China from western countries, and second to enter India in the future. The British army was in Burma at that time and fought the Japanese army. The Chinese detachment went to Burma to assist the British army and secure the supply lines.

The Chinese detachment went into Burma in 1942, but at first was defeated by the Japanese army. A section of it escaped to India and was trained there by US advisors, and the other section returned to the western Yunnan province. Both sections would attack the Japanese army in Burma when they were ready.

On October 24, 1943, the 112th regiment of the new 38th division began to attack the Japanese army and on October 29, took Shinbwinyang and entered Hukawng Valley. When the Japanese army there found the regiment, they surrounded it. In resistance, the regiment lived on Japanese bananas and on food delivered by air drops. The Japanese army could not break through their defense. On November 24, the new 38th division came to assist and on November 29, they took the position of the Japanese army, who lost round 1,000 soldiers.

The campaign continued in January 1944, when the Japanese

army receded into the valley and made their defensive line at Dalou and Tabajia. The Chinese new 38th division came to attack Tabajia, and the new 22nd division came to attack Dalou. At dawn on January 28, the American air force came to bombard the Japanese position at Dalou and the tanks of the new 22nd division ran through the Japanese defensive line. The new 22nd division took all the fortresses outside Dalou. On January 31 Chinese tanks entered Dalou and crushed the Japanese headquarters. On that day, the new 38th division attacked Tabajia. The American air force raided the Japanese army there, who had to retreat. On the 1st of February, the new 38th division occupied Tabajia.

The Japanese army retreated to Mengguan and Walupan, 8 miles apart. They wanted to induce the Chinese army to attack Walupan so that another section of their army could attack from the back. The new 22nd division assaulted Mengguan with artillery and tanks. The new 38th division stationed at the left rear to protect its back. The Japanese section came to attack the new 22th division from behind, but was blocked by the new 38th division. As the new 22nd division attacked for a week and could not secure the place, the new 38th division sent its 113th regiment to attack Walupan to distract the attention of the Japanese army. On March 1, the American 5307 corps reached them and launched their onslaught. So the 22nd division broke through the Japanese defensive line. On the 4th of March, the new 22nd division took Mengguan. Now the Japanese army was surrounded in the narrow strip of Walupan. At noon of the 8th of March, the Chinese army and the American corps jointly attacked Walupan and took it on the 9th of March. Thus ended the campaign in this area.

The campaigns in the western Hunan province

After the outbreak of the Pacific War, the US air force helped China to fight Japan. Towards the termination of the Sino–Japanese War, the Americans got the upper hand over the Japanese air force. American bombers raided important Japanese military bases, including airports. More than once, the American fighter planes engaged Japanese fighter planes in the air and gained victory. There was an airport for US airplanes at the Zhijiang in the western Hunan province. The goal of Japan at the start of this campaign in 1945 was to capture the airport. It was the last major battle in the Sino–Japanese War.

On April 9, 1945, the Japanese 47th military bloc and the 116th bloc started their onslaught at Lantian. The commander of the Chinese defensive 73rd army in that area estimated that the Japanese army had not finished pulling together its forces. And so he gave orders to launch a surprise attack. The Japanese 47th bloc suffered the blow, and later when it was ready, the 47th bloc began to cross the Zi River on April 14. The Chinese commander let the Japanese cross the river, but as most of the Japanese army was reaching the bank of this side of the river, the Chinese army struck them with artillery while American airplanes attacked those Japanese soldiers still on the boat. Many boats were sunken. The Japanese army had a heavy loss.

On April 28, the Japanese 116th bloc was surrounded by the Chinese army and signaled to the 47th bloc for rescue. When the 47th bloc arrived, they could not break the Chinese 73rd army's defense. On the 30th day, the Chinese army fought back and defeated the enemy, aided by air raids. The Japanese army had to retreat back to where they had come from. The battle ended in this district, but the warfare still continued in other districts.

On the 12th of April, the Japanese 34th bloc had attacked Xinning. A Chinese battalion under the 58th division of the 74th Army fought them for three days. Then as the Japanese reinforcements came, the battalion had to withdraw from Xinning, which was taken by the Japanese army. On April 21, 4,000 Japanese soldiers marched towards Meikou. On April 23, they began to cross the Wushui River. The Chinese 44th division waited there patiently till the first 200 Japanese soldiers set foot on the bank. Then they fell on them fiercely and slew them all. The Japanese kept on crossing, but had to stop under heavy cannon fire. On April 27, they turned to attack Wuyang, and after two days' fighting, they took half of Wuyang. On April 29 the Chinese 44th division came and the Japanese army had to give up the attack and turn back to fight the 44th division, who soon put the Japanese army to rout.

On April 27, another Japanese detachment attacked Wugan, which was an old town. The walls were very strong, because the bricks were stuck together using sticky rice cooked in water, which became glue. Many ancient tombs were also built this way to prevent them from being dug through. So when the Japanese cannon balls exploded and hit the walls, the shards did little damage to the walls. On May 1, the Japanese formed suicide squads, but the soldiers, who had not reached the wall yet, were killed by gunfire from the battlements. At last, some soldiers got to the wall and blew a hole in it with dynamite. However, the Chinese people, who helped their soldiers in the defense of the town, heaved bags filled with sand down on the spot and the hole was blocked by the sand bags. Then the Japanese army used long wooden siege ladders. But the Chinese army used flame throwers, provided to them by the United States, to burn the ladders. For seven days the Chinese soldiers, aided by civilians, kept the small ancient town safe and sound. The Japanese army was defeated by the Chinese reinforcements.

Other battles also took place in other districts in the western Hunan province. The whole campaign ended on June 2 with the failure of the Japanese army.

Failure or victory in war mostly depends on two factors: how strong are the forces and how wise are the strategies used. But oftentimes, using a very wise ruse, the weaker side can defeat the stronger and the few fighters can defeat greater forces.

Building the Communist Ranks in YanAn

Gathering students

After the XiAn event at the end of 1936, the Central Committee of the Communist Party moved in January of 1937 to YanAn, a small backward town in the north of Shaanxi province. At that time, Chiang Kai-shek would not come to fight them anymore as they had an agreement. Therefore, the Communist Party was ready to gather lots of people with intelligence and talent, no matter young or middle aged. Their party members in big cities, where the most intelligent and talented people generally lived, adopted every possible means to allure such people, especially young students, to YanAn to serve the Communist Party. Young people were easier to entice than middle-aged ones. So many young people went to YanAn, thinking that they could be trained to fight the Japanese invaders. Most young people went there in 1937, 1938, and 1939. Later many of those who became communist cadres were those who had gone there in 1938. So '38 cadres became a special name for those.

The Communist Party founded a so-called Anti-Japanese military and political university and some schools to mentally train the students to become communist cadres. Yue Shan, a student in Duize high school in Changsha city, recalled that one day in 1938, Xu Deli, a Communist Party member and a representative of Changsha bureau of the 8th Route Army, came to give a speech about the Japanese invasion and called on young people to go to YanAn. His speech was so touching that Yue Shan and some other students enrolled on the spot.

Duan Xuesheng, a Communist Party member and a writer, worked in Shandong province as a teacher, and propagandized to students about communism and instigated them to go to YanAn to take part in the revolution. In Suiyang province and inner Mongolian district, more than 100 young people were attracted to YanAn. In Peking, from May to August in 1938, 107 young people decided to go.

The Central Committee of the Communist Party set up 8th Route Army bureaus in many towns and cities to enroll young people, especially students, to go to YanAn. Statistics showed that the bureau in Lanzhou of Gansu province sent 3,000 in the autumn of 1937. The bureau in Wuhan sent 880 from March to May in 1938. Chongqing sent 2,000. However, those who were permitted to go to YanAn had to have three interviews. Everyone had to produce a letter of recommendation from an organization established by the Communist Party in the place he or she lived. The last interview was held by the organization department of the Central Committee of the Communist Party.

The tide of young people flowing to YanAn caused concern in the Nationalist Party. Chiang Kai-shek ordered these young people to be detained. In Yanyang, 103 students were detained by the military police of the Nationalist government. After more than ten days, 40 students were carried away in a truck and others were still in custody. In November 1939, labor camps were set up to confine all the students on the way to YanAn. They were assailed with counter-propaganda and "mentally trained" until they expressed their loyalty to the Nationalist government, and then they were freed. By the end of 1940, 1,167 students had been detained in the labor camps. From 1939 to 1943, 2,100 students were taken into custody on their way to YanAn.

By the end of 1943, there were 40,000 young newcomers in YanAn, and half of them were female. Many of the females married high-ranking cadres of the Communist Party. Those of the cadres who had already married village girls deserted their wives when they entered big cities like Beijing after 1949, and simply married young city girls.

A special case must be mentioned. Wen Lianchen, alias Xia Sha, a girl of 14 at the time, was the daughter of a town mayor. When the family was in Wuhan, she stole out of the house and wanted to go to YanAn, but was stopped in a train and taken home by a friend of her father's at Zhengzhou. When the family moved to Chongqing, she insisted on going to YanAn. Her father could do nothing but let her go. He bought a plane ticket for her to XiAn. She found the 8th Route Army bureau there and was safely sent to YanAn. This was the only case when someone went to YanAn by plane.

Jiang Qing—Mao Zedong's 4th wife —in Yanan

Jiang Qing (1914–1991) was born in Zhu Town of Shandong province. Her original name was Li Yunhe. Her father Li Dewen ran a carpentry shop. Her mother was his concubine, who had been a maidservant. In the summer of 1921, Li Yunhe was in primary school, but in 1926, she was expelled. Her father died of some disease in the same year and her mother took her to live with her brother-in-law in Tianjin city; he was an officer in the army of the warlord Zhang Zuolin. Jiang Qing had worked for three months as a child laborer in the factory of the British–American Tobacco Co., Ltd. In 1928, the brother-in-law moved his troops somewhere else, and her mother took her to live with her cousin in JiNan. In spring of 1929, when she was 15 years old, she learned to be an actress in a theater in the city. In May of 1931, she married a man from a wealthy family, but got divorced in July. Then she went to Qingdao, and from July of 1931 to April of 1933, she worked in a library there. But in February of 1932, at the age 18, she was living with (not married to) Yu Qiwei, three years older than she, a university student majoring in biography, who was also the leader of the propaganda department of the Communist Party there. He had contact with those in the circles of so-called communist culture.

Li Yunhe had acted in a one-scene play named *Put Down Your*

Whip, which could be performed in the street as a protest against the Japanese aggression. In February of 1933, she took an oath and joined the Communist Party through Yu Qiwei in a warehouse in Qingdao. In April, Yu was arrested and she ran away to Shanghai. In May, she attended "The Great China University" by auditing classes. In July she worked as a music teacher in a primary school in the western suburb of Shanghai and acted in some amateur plays after work. In September of 1934, she was arrested, but in February 1935, she was released and went to Peking to live with Yu Qiwei again, who had been released, too.

But in March, she returned to Shanghai to join the Diantong Film Company, using her stage name Lanping. She acted the heroine in the play *Nara*, and got good reviews. Afterwards, she played roles in two movies. In September, she was living with Tanner, a movie reviewer. In April of 1936, she was married to him. The ceremony was held together with two other couples, before Liuhe Pagoda in Hangzhou, in the moonlight. A romantic ritual.

Jiang Qing & Tanner, the middle couple of the front row

However, she still kept in touch with Yu Qiwei and by July Tanner could not bear it; he failed in an attempted suicide. She went back to Shanghai and joined the Lianhua Film Company. She had a role in the film *Blood on Wolf Mountain*. In February of 1937, she acted in the drama *Thunderstorm*. On the 30th of May, Tanner attempted suicide again, but still to no avail. Afterwards he went to France and lived there forever.

In September of 1937, as the Anti-Japanese War broke out, Li Yunhe left Shanghai and in August, she arrived in YanAn and changed her name to Jiang Qing. In November, she was enrolled in the Anti-Japanese Military and Political University. On the 10th of April, 1938, the Lu Xun Arts College was founded and she was appointed instructor of the drama department. She acted in two dramas, and in August acted in a Peking opera. Her efforts were appreciated and soon afterwards, she was promoted to secretary in the office of the military committee, close to Mao. It was said that she often went to see Mao and asked for instructions from him. This intimacy changed their relationship and soon she was living with Mao in place of his current wife He Zizhen, who was studying in Moscow at the time. In 1939, Mao married her. But at the time, she had not been divorced from Tanner yet and Mao had not been divorced from He Zizhen. Both committed bigamy.

Quite a few Communist Party leaders opposed the marriage, Zhang Wentian first and foremost. He maintained that He Zizhen was a good comrade and must be respected as a legal wife. Besides, she had been wounded in the Long March and could not be ignored like this. Wang Shiying had been in Shanghai and knew all about Jiang Qing's love affairs, which were really scandals. And as the leader of the Communist Party, Mao should not marry a woman with such a background. So he wrote a letter outlining these scandals. He asked Nan Hanchen to sign the letter, too, who also worked in Shanghai and knew about it all. (Both were later persecuted to death by Jiang Qing in the Cultural Revolution.) Only Kang Sheng (1898–1975) supported their marriage.

Then the Communist Party had a meeting and put up three conditions: 1) Jiang Qing should not interfere in political affairs;

2) Jiang Qing could not take up any office, inside or outside the Communist Party; 3) Jiang Qing's main task was to look after Mao in his health and personal life.

Jiang Qing had a daughter with Mao, born in 1940 and called Li Na, who is still alive now, in retirement.

Mao's marriage history and his other women

Mao had four formal marriages. His first wife was Ms. Luo (no given name known), whom Mao married in accordance with arrangements made by his parents. She was then 20 years old while Mao was only 16. The Mao family and Luo family were relatives. Though she was a pleasant woman, Mao did not like her. They married in 1907. But in February of 1910, she died of some disease. Using this as a pretext, Mao left his family and went to Peking.

His second wife was Yang Kaihui (1901–1930), whose father, Yang Changji, was a graduate returned from England who became a professor of ethics at Peking University. At that time Mao worked in the library and studied as a guest student. He and Yang Kaihui were classmates. In 1919, Mao began to court Yang Kaihui, and in 1920, they lived together without legally marrying. At that time Mao was 26 years old and Yang was only 18. She bore three sons for Mao. In 1921, Yang joined the Communist Party, but afterwards she was arrested by the Nationalist government and was executed on the 14th of November, 1930. Her first son, Mao Anying (1922–1950), died in the Korean War. Her second son, Mao Anqing (1923–2007), was escorted by Kang Sheng to Moscow. He joined the Communist Party in 1947. In July of 1949, he was given the rank of Lieutenant Colonel, but he was engaged in research work in the Academy of Military Sciences, not combat. He died of heart disease. Yang's third son, Mao Anlong, was a riddle. It was said that he went missing as a child and no one knew what became of him even now. And no one ever appeared claiming that he was Mao's third son.

Mao's third wife was He Zizhen (1910–1984), sister of marshal He Long. In 1927 when Mao went to Jinggang Mountain after the riot, he met He Zizhen there. That year, Mao was 35 years old while she was only 17. In June of 1928, they got married while his second wife Yang Kaihui was in prison. It has never been said that Mao had endeavored to rescue her from the prison. When He Zizhen grew up, she became the secretary of the frontier committee of the Red Army and director of the women's league in the southwestern Jiangxi province. In the Long March, while protecting the wounded soldiers from air raids, she was wounded herself. In January of 1938, she went to study in Moscow and returned to China in the summer of 1947. Then she took up offices like director of the women's league in Hangzhou city. He Zizhen had her first child with Mao in 1929, and when they had to escape, He Zizhen left her daughter with a local family. The child was called Mao Jinhua. In April, 1932, when He Zizhen wanted to find the child, she was told that the child had died. In fact, the child did not die. At that time some agents of the Nationalist Party had come to inquire about the child and so the adoptive family lied, saying the child had died, lest they kill it. The child grew up and was named Yang Yuehua. In 1973, an old Red Army man came to the place and learned something about Yang Yuehua and he notified He Zizhen's brother, who informed his sister of the truth. However, it was during the Cultural Revolution when Jiang Qing was in power, so the mother and the daughter could not see each other. The daughter is alive now in retirement. He zizhen had another daughter called Mao Jiaojiao. But afterwards when Mao Zedong changed his name to Li Desheng to avoid being arrested by the Nationalist government, this daughter changed her name to Li Min, which is used till now. He Zizhen died in Shanghai at the age 75.

His fourth wife was Jiang Qing (see above). But he had many other women outside of marriage. The first one we know about was Tao Siyong, from a rich family. She was known as a woman of talent and a beauty, too. From 1919 to 1920, she and Mao opened a bookstore in Changsha. Mao wrote many love letters to her. Five of them were found later. In 1921, she went to study in Jinling College in Nanking. As her father did not like Mao, she did not marry him. She died in 1931 at the age of 36 without marrying anyone. The next one was Ding Ling, a so-called red writer. She was born on the 12th of October, 1904. She was a classmate of Yang Kaihui in high school. She joined the Communist Party in 1932 and was arrested too, but in September of 1936, with the assistance of the Communist Party, escaped from prison in Nanking and went to YanAn. Mao loved her at first sight. She was the chief editor of *Journal of Literature and Arts*, and then the party secretary of the Chinese Writers Association, and the chief editor of *People's Literature*, etc. But in the anti-rightist movement in 1957, she was declared a rightist and was exiled to a cold region in northeastern China. She died on March 4, 1986.

Another was Wu Lili, born in 1912. She went to America for further studies after graduation from the Normal University in Peking. When she learned of the outbreak of the Anti-Japanese, she came back to China, to YanAn, to fight Japan. She became Mao's interpreter and they fell in love. But when He Zizhen heard about this, she went there and caught them together. She wanted to kill them both. This became such a big scandal that the Central Committee of the Communist Party had to intervene. Wu Lili was sent away. Afterwards, she married an officer of the Nationalist Party and went to live in Taiwan.

Sun Weishi was also one, whose father was a fellow fighter of Premier Zhou. When he died in 1927, Sun Weishi was only 5. So Premier Zhou took care of her and looked upon her as his adopted daughter, but openly known as his niece. Then she went with Zhou Enlai to YanAn. She was called the red princess. In 1939, she went with Zhou Enlai to Moscow to study drama. In December 1949, Mao went to the Soviet Union with Zhou; Sun Weishi was their interpreter and also taught Mao some Russian. Mao had a carriage of his own in the train. One night Mao raped her in his carriage. Sun told Zhou about it, but Zhou did not dare to say anything. In the Cultural Revolution, her brother was tragically beaten to death and Sun wrote to Jiang Qing to ask for an investigation. She also wrote to Zhou. Both without result. In December 1967, her husband was put in prison on spying charges. Her home was searched and some letters to Mao were found. Jiang Qing took these letters to see Zhou Enlai and blamed him for it. Jiang even slapped Zhou's face in wrath. Zhou could not do anything to her. Before long Sun Weishi was put in a secret prison on the orders of Jiang Qing and was tortured to death. A long nail was driven into her head. Jiang Qing wanted Zhou Enlai to sign an order to execute Sun Weishi; Zhou did not dare to refuse and signed it. No comment needed here.

Feng Fengming was a returned overseas Chinese and was

talented in drama. When she arrived in YanAn, she was enrolled in the Lu Xun Arts College and then became an actress. One day after a performance, Mao invited her to his place to discuss acting. Then and there, he violated her. She was so infuriated that she left YanAn. No one knew where she went.

In 1962, Mao went to Shanghai. The mayor Ke Qingshi at the time made arrangements for Mao to meet the famous movie star Shangguan Yunzhu. A friend of hers had witnessed a note Mao had written to Shangguan. Mao wrote that "A hero loved a beauty since the olden days. I am the hero. You are the beauty." The next year, Mao came to Shanghai again and met her again. Every time, they would stay together for several days. In 1965, she was brought to Zhongnanhai (literally, central south sea) in Beijing, where Mao lived. They openly lived together. Not long later, Mao took her back to Shanghai and she never saw him again. In 1966, she was arrested under orders of Jiang Qing and she died in jail.

In Mao's late years, Zhang Yufeng worked as Mao's secretary and looked after him day and night. Zhang was born in 1944 to a poor family in northeastern China. In 1958, Zhang worked as a train attendant. Then she was transferred to the special train for Mao in 1962. In 1967, she was married to a man working in the railway department. But in July 1970, Mao took a liking to her and she was sent to work in Zhongnanhai. She looked after Mao's health and daily life. She lived with Mao till his death. Then she moved out of Zhongnanhai. Now she's enjoying a quiet retired life.

The Puppet Governments in China Under Japan

The assassination of Wang Jingwei

Japan knew that for such a big country as China, they would need to set up some puppet governments as they could not rule all China by themselves. Manchukuo in the northeastern China was the first puppet government Japan established. As Japan expanded into other provinces, they founded other local puppet governments. From December 1937 to March 1938, puppet governments were set up in Peking and in Nanking.

Japan always wanted to induce Chiang Kai-shek and the

Nationalist government to surrender to Japan and became the central puppet government, but never succeeded. In November, 1938, Japan sent someone to talk to Wang Jingwei and his clique. His two important followers were Chen Gongbo (1892–1946) and Zhou Fohai (1897–1948). Both were originally members of the Communist Party. It was said that most of the members of any party were mainly opportunists. They would go where personal benefits beckoned to them.

Wang always wanted to be the head of a government, but he was no rival to Chiang Kai-shek who controlled the army. Now Japan offered him a chance to be one, though only the head of a puppet government. Better than nothing. So the representatives of both sides had a secret talk in Shanghai and signed an agreement stating that the new government recognized Manchukuo, and that Japan had priority over any natural resources in China, etc. On the 18th of December, 1938, Wang Jingwei, Chen Gongbo and Zhou Fohai stealthily left Chongqing, the temporary wartime capital, and went to Kunming, where they took a plane to Hanoi in Vietnam.

On December 29, 1938, Wang sent out a public telegram stating three points as his principles for negotiating with Japan: firstly, be friendly to the adjacent countries; secondly, to cooperate with Japan against the Communist Party; thirdly, to get financial assistance from Japan. The Nationalist government and the Communist Party both saw Wang's statement as a betrayal of China and a capitulation to Japan. So Wang and his followers were defined as traitors.

Therefore, on New Year's Day of 1939, Chiang Kai-shek had a meeting to announce that Wang was expelled from the Nationalist Party and dismiss from all his offices. Next he planned to get rid of Wang physically. Some special agents were sent to assassinate him in Hanoi.

Wang and his wife, Chen Bijun, and another follower, hid in a house and seldom went out. The special agents were composed of 18 experienced assassins, called "18 Arhans," which came from the Buddhist culture, but meant "strong men" in Chinese culture. They arrived in Hanoi and got all the information they needed about Wang, and where he lived. They were waiting for the final order from Chiang Kai-shek. Chiang still harbored a hope that

Wang would turn back to the Nationalist government. He sent an emissary to Hanoi to have a talk with Wang, but Wang refused the request to go back. Wang and his wife knew that they were now in danger of being killed.

On the 19th of March, Chiang Kai-shek gave the final order to rid of Wang. So the 18 Arhans got ready for action. At 9 o'clock on the 20th day, when the agents had a meeting to arrange for the action, they heard that Wang and his men were getting ready to leave the house. So the agents came to chase them, riding in two cars. When Wang and his men found that they were being followed, they succeeded in shaking the agents off in the heavy traffic at an intersection.

At 4 o'clock the next day, Wang's new location was disclosed. So six agents went there. They had to act fast because they were in a foreign country. Vietnam at that time was under French rule. Wang's guards could not carry guns. But the agents secretly had guns carried in. So when the agents attacked, the guards were defenseless. One agent went to the room where Want was supposed to be. The agent used an ax to make a hole in the door and saw a man and a woman inside. He shot at the man three times. He witnessed the bullets hit home and left as fast as he could. Three of the agents escaped and three of them were arrested by the police in Hanoi. Afterwards, while they were happy thinking that they had finished off Wang, information arrived that Wang was still alive. Only one of his followers was killed. Some of the agents left and some remained behind for further action. But they never killed Wang.

The puppet government in Nanking

On March 27, Wang published an article revealing the minutes of a Nationalist government meeting where the conditions of peace proposed by Japan were discussed. And Chiang Kai-shek basically agreed to the conditions. Wang wanted to show to Chinese people and the world that Chiang Kai-shek was the first to negotiate with Japan, not he. But he did not know the difference there. Chiang Kai-shek only wanted to negotiate with Japan for a truce while Wang himself was ready to surrender to Japan.

On March 22, the Japanese general consulate reported to the

Japanese government about the assassination attempt on Wang. On March 25, Wang and his men went on board a French ship under the protection of Japan and then were transferred to a Japanese ship. He arrived in Shanghai on the 6th of May. Then Wang went to Tokyo to have a talk with the prime minister about the establishment of a central puppet government in China. On the 30th of March, 1940, the puppet government was founded in Nanking, with Wang at its head.

Japan called it the Nanking national government, but Chiang Kai-shek refused to recognize it. But Germany, Italy, Hungary, Romania, Denmark, Spain, Croatia, Slovakia, and Bulgaria recognized it. The puppet government imitated the Nationalist government in organization and had its own puppet army, which was thus called by people. But the puppet army took orders from the Japanese army, not directly from the Wang and his men. The puppet government did everything under the supervision and command of Japan, just like the Manchurian puppet emperor in northeastern China.

In March of 1944, Wang was very ill and went to Japan for treatment. On the 10th of November, he died in the hospital there. Then Chen Gongbo, one of the founders of the CPC, became the head of the puppet government. When Japan surrendered in 1945, Chen Gongbo and his wife flew to Japan but were extradited to China October 3. He and Chen Bijun, the wife of Wang, were put in prison in February of 1946 in Suzhou. On the 4th of June, Chen Gongbo was executed. Chen Bijun was sentenced to life and died in prison on the 17th of June, 1959. She pleaded for herself, saying that she had wanted to save the nation in an indirect way. "Trying to save the nation in an indirect way" was a common term of ridicule thereafter.

As for Zhou Fohai, another founding member of the CPC, when he sensed that Japan would soon perish, he secretly made contact with Chiang Kai-shek and the Nationalists. After the victory, Chiang Kai-shek appointed him as commander-in-chief to maintain law and order in Nanking and Shanghai till the Nationalist government army came. But on the September 30, 1945, he was apprehended and sent to Chongqing, then brought back to Nanking. On October 21, his case was tried in court, and on November 7, he was sentenced to death. But in March of 1947,

Chiang Kai-shek issued an order of amnesty for him, and the sentence was commuted to life imprisonment. He died of heart disease in the jail on February 28, 1948.

The rectification campaign of the Communist Party in yanan

Besides the 8th Route Army, the new 4th army was also under the control of the Communist Party. The new 4th army had their position in the southern Anhui province. So the Communist Party had two armies of their own, one in the northwest and the other in the southeast. Mao always hated Chiang Kai-shek and had once planned to attack Chiang Kai-shek from behind with 150,000 men. But the plan was aborted when the Communist International objected to it. In 1941, an incident flared up between the new 4th army and the 32nd military bloc of the Nationalist government.

On the night January 4, 1941, 9,000 of the new 4th army under the command of Xiang Yin maneuvered from the southern Anhui province to the north side of the Yangtze River through the southern Jiangsu province, without notifying the Nationalist government. The National 32nd bloc thought that the new 4th army was trying to attack their 40th division, and on January 6, they surrounded it and assailed it. Several times, Xiang Yin telegrammed YanAn, but Mao never answered or gave any instruction what to do. On January 10, the new 4th army telegrammed Mao again. On January 12, Mao asked Zhou Enlai to protest to the Nationalist government and request the withdrawal of their army. So the next day, Zhou protested to the Nationalist government. The fight had already been going on for seven days. of the 9,000 soldiers in the new 4th army, only 2,000 escaped.

After the incident, Mao decided that the Communist Party of China should not follow the guidance of the Communist International any more. They should make decisions on their own. Therefore, the Communist Party launched a rectification campaign, which is considered to have begun in May 1941 when Mao made a speech, "Reform Our Studies." In June, the propaganda department of the Central Committee of the Communist Party issued a document, "Instruction concerning how to wage the campaign of studies and rectification within the whole party." But the campaign actually started in February, 1942, when Mao made another speech, "Rectify Our Style of Work," and it ended when a bill was passed in a session of the Central Committee of the Communist Party, "The resolution of some historical problems," in April 1945.

However, what really happened in the rectification campaign was that everyone had to make some kind of confession about their inner thoughts to show loyalty to the party. Many people who had come to YanAn from the regions under the Nationalist government were suspected of being spies of the Nationalist Party. Many of those were forced to confess that they were indeed spies sent by the Nationalist Party. If they wanted to be punished less severely, they had to expose others who were also spies. Mao hinted that to achieve this purpose, some harsh measures would be necessary. The most common method was not to let the one being cross-examined get any sleep. It was called fatigue-torture. In American it's called sleep deprivation. Another method was to let those suspects watch someone being shot; just a little psychological pressure.

In April 1943 alone, several thousand people were put under custody. Some were locked up in caves. Some were just confined to their work places—"equivalent prisons," they called them. There were not enough jailers to watch over the prisoners, so their colleagues assumed the task. This was a clever invention of Mao. To show their loyalty to the party, the colleagues had to do their duties faithfully and keep watch over the prisoners. No one could escape their vigilance. About a thousand people died. Some committed suicide. To them this was not a political movement, but terrorism. Many people who had come to YanAn in hopes of fighting Japan died at the hands of their own comrades.

On August 15, 1943, Mao said that in such campaigns, some errors were unavoidable (like a bit of torture). The errors should not be corrected too early, or there would be no targets and that would hinder the development of the campaign. If the errors were corrected too late, people would be very upset and it would cause too much loss. So the principle was to watch the campaign closely, calculating accurately, and stop it at the right time.

As it became more apparent that Japan was likely to lose the war, Mao liberated those prisoners who luckily had survived and who, in Mao's calculation, could be sent to fight Chiang Kai-shek after the victory. To assuage their enmity, Mao apologized several times, saying that the aim of the rectification campaign was to let them have a political bath to wash off the dust they carried from the regions under Chiang's government, but too much potassium permanganate (which can cause caustic burns) was used, which had hurt the tender skin of the new comers. He added that if a son was beaten by the father, he should not hate his father.

CHAPTER 4. THE SECOND CIVIL WAR BETWEEN THE NATIONALIST PARTY AND THE COMMUNIST PARTY

Conflicts Between the Two Parties to Take Over Areas Occupied By Japan

After Japan surrendered, there arose a problem as to who would take over the areas that had been occupied by the Japanese army. The Nationalist Party thought that they were the legal government and had the right to these areas. Afraid that the Communist Party would take those areas when the Japanese army withdrew, the Nationalist government ordered the Japanese army to remain in the areas they occupied till the army of the Nationalist government came to take them. However, the Communist Party declared that they had the right to these areas. So regardless of any orders from the Nationalist government, they marched to some of the areas controlled by Japan and took over by force.

Now, most of the Nationalist government army was in the southwestern provinces and part of it was stationed to south of the Yangtze River. Almost no Nationalist Army forces were in the areas north of the Yangtze river. And the army of the Communist Party spread widely in the countryside north of the River and in the northeastern provinces. But when the Communist Army commanded the Japanese army to surrender to them, the Japanese army refused as they had received orders not to surrender to the Communist Army. Therefore, the Communist Army had to fight the Japanese army and the puppet army to occupy towns possessed by the Japanese army.

Even before Japan surrendered, the Nationalist government and the Soviet Union signed a treaty stipulating that the Nationalist government recognized the independence of Outer Mongolia (as the Chinese called it), and the special rights of the Soviet Union in northeastern China, in exchange for the Soviet Union's promise not to support the Communist Army in occupying the northeastern provinces. From then on, Outer Mongolia became the Mongolian Republic and Inner Mongolia still belonged to China.

From August 14–23, Chiang Kai-shek telegrammed Mao three times to invite him to Chongqing to talk about the future of China. On August 25, the Communist Party issued a declaration that the Nationalist government must recognize the government in YanAn (denoting the local red government of the Communist Party) and its army in the so-called liberated areas as lawful, and that all the parties were legal and would have to organize a joint government. On August 26, the Communist Party decided that Mao should go to Chongqing to negotiate. But the talks did not produce an agreement, especially about who would take over all the areas occupied by the Japanese army. So while the talks were going on, the fighting was going at the same time. For the Communist Party, when they attacked the Japanese army and the puppet army to take over towns in their possession, they had to fight the Nationalist Army as well, as both wanted to take the same town.

By August 26, the Communist Army took 59 towns from the hands of the Japanese. Then under orders from the Nationalist government, the Japanese army and the puppet army attacked the Communist Army and restored more than 20 towns by the end of September. The Communist Army changed their original plan; they gave up the eastern part of the Ping-Han railway line and concentrated on the northern provinces. So many of the Communist Army set out for the north and by the end of November, more than 100,000 communist soldiers reached north-eastern China, the farthest place, where the Nationalist Army could not arrive ahead of them.

On the 10th of September, the Communist Army attacked several towns under control of the Nationalist government in Shanxi province and took most of them within ten days. Then they surrounded Tunliu. The national defensive army in Chang-zhi sent 6,000 soldiers to Tunliu, but they were blocked on the way by a communist detachment. This strategy was often used by the Communist Army to surround some place and lay an ambush along the likely approach route by which reinforcements would come. So the Nationalist Army from Changzhi could not go to Tunliu and had to return to Changzhi. On September 12, the Communist Army took Tunliu and came to surround Chang-zhi. On the 2nd of October, a Nationalist reinforcements went to Chingzhi, and as usual, encountered a communist detachment who came out of ambush and surrounded them. As the communist detachment met with strong resistance, they adopted another stratagem. They surrounded the Nationalist reinforce-ments from three sides, leaving one side open for them to escape, and laid another ambush down that way. The reinforcements did escape, only to fall into the second ambush, and was wiped out on the 5th of October. This ruse was often used in Chinese war history. It was not invented by the Communist Party.

On the 10th of October, after lengthy peace talks, the Nation-alist Party and the Communist Party at last signed an agreement, called the 10/10 agreement, which contained the articles to form a joint government, to nationalize the armies of both sides, and to implement democracy and constitutionalism.

Although the peace agreement was signed, the Communist Party still planned to stop the Nationalist Army from going to the northern areas to accept the surrender of the Japanese army there. They looked upon the northern areas as belonging to them, and considered the Nationalist Army to be trespassing if they went there.

On the 20th of October, when the Nationalist Army arrived at Zhuang River, on the way to Handan, and on October 22 crossed the river, the Communist Army was waiting for them. On Octo-ber 24, the Nationalist Army broke through the blockade and reached Matou town in a narrow valley where they were encircled by the Communist Army. On October 28, more Communist Army troops came and they began the attack. At the same time the Communist Party sent an envoy to see the commander of the new 8th army of the Nationalist government and persuaded him to betray the Nationalist government. On October 30, the new 8th army declared their insurrection. On October 31, the main National forces broke the encirclement of the Communist Army and escaped south. From October of 1945 to January of 1946, the Communist Army occupied Jinpu railway line, Longhai railway line, Jiaoji railway line, and all the towns along the three lines. These areas had strategic importance and were threats to the safety of Nanking and Shanghai.

America's mediation between the Nationalist Party and the Communist Party

After the outbreak of the Pacific war, beginning with the Japanese raid of the Pearl Harbor, America aided China a lot, in both military action and supplies of goods. Joseph Stilwell, chief of staff of the Allies, came to China. His main job was to guarantee that the supplies needed in the Anti-Japanese war reached the hands of the Nationalist Army through the highway from Burma to Yunnan province.

At the request of the Allies, in early 1942, the Nationalist government sent its army into Burma, where it would be under the command of Joseph Stilwell to aid the English army. But when the Chinese army reached Burma, the English army there was already defeated by Japan. Then the Japanese army surrounded the Chinese army, which, nevertheless, succeeded afterwards in breaking through the encirclement, and separated into two parts. The first part, under orders from Joseph Stilwell, went to India, and the second part returned to Yunnan province through the virgin forest. The international supplies were mostly used in the Burmese battlefields and only a few reached the Nationalist government. Chiang Kai-shek was dissatisfied with this and also with the failure of the Chinese army under the command of Joseph Stilwell in the Burmese war. Therefore, in 1943, Chiang asked twice for Stilwell to be replaced. But Chiang did not succeed because of the opposition of Alfred Marshall in the United States.

After the spring of 1944, the withdrawal of the Nationalist Army after the Japanese army attack made President Roosevelt send his vice president Wallace to China to see what was the real situation. Wallace was not impressed with the Nationalist government of China. In August, three times, President Roosevelt asked Chiang Kai-shek to give the command of the Chinese army to Stilwell, but Chiang replied that if he had to give up his command of the army to Stilwell, he would rather break off relations with the Allies and fight Japan with Chinese forces alone. At length, after consideration, President Roosevelt gave order to replace Stilwell and appointed Wedemeyer for the task, on the 18th of October, 1944.

Meantime, with the quick development of the communist forces, an American delegation headed by Colonel Barrett went to YanAn, in July of 1944, followed on the 7th of November, 1944, by Patrick Jay Hurley, American ambassador in China, who went to YanAn to talk about the legal status of the Communist Party. They reached an agreement to end the dictatorship and one-party rule, to include all the parties in the Anti-Japanese war in the joint national government, to recognize the legal status of all the parties, and to distribute all the supplies among them.

Patrick Jay Hurley came back to Chongqing and had a conversation with Chiang Kai-shek, who had three conditions: 1) the Nationalist government recognized the lawful status of the Communist Party and would reorganize its army; 2) the Communist Party must give the command of its army to the military committee of the Nationalist government and the Nationalist government would appoint some generals of the Communist Party as members of the military committee; 3) the aim of the Nationalist government was to realize Three Principles of the People. of course, two conditions were denied by the Communist Party. They could never yield the command of their army to anyone else, and their aim was to install communism. But in face, no one in the Communist Party knew what communism really was. They mainly used it as a slogan to mislead people.

After Japan's surrender, the Communist Party and the Nationalist Party fought each other over the areas occupied by Japan. To appease both sides, Hurley suggested Chiang Kai-shek invite Mao to Chongqing for a talk. Though Mao came, the fight continued. The Communist Party, supported by the Soviet Union, took the initiative to attack the Nationalist Army. On November 26th, 1945, Hurley handed in his resignation to President Truman. Fearful of a civil war in China, President Truman sent Alfred Marshall there, who arrived in Shanghai on the 20th of December, 1945.

Alfred Marshall talked to both sides and then formed a trio group. Besides Alfred Marshall, Zhang Jun represented the Nationalist Party and Zhou Enlai the Communist Party. On the 10th of January, 1946, they reached an agreement for truce, effective at zero hour on the 13th of January. Both sides issued orders for a ceasefire.

On the 5th of January, Chiang Kai-shek made a suggestion to Alfred Marshall about how to reorganize the army of both sides. On January 23, a trio group discussed it. Alfred Marshall suggested that after the reorganization, there would be only 60 divisions, 20 of them under the communist command. As to the navy and air forces, the Communist Party would have 30% of each. Chiang did not consent to that, but made some concessions. However, on 25th, the trio signed an agreement. Then they flew to Peking and YanAn to oversee the preparations.

On the 11th of March, Marshall went back to the States. The two parties went back to war. When Marshall came to China again on April 18, the situation was serious. Chiang Kai-shek told Marshall that the Communist Party would not abide by the agreement and was continuing its attack on Changchun city. Chiang added that the Nationalist Army might withdraw from the northeastern provinces and leave the problem up to the international parties to decide. Marshall promised to transport the 60th Nationalist Army and the 93rd Nationalist Army to those provinces, but he refused to have two more armies transported there. (If two more armies had been transported there, China might have had a different future. Was this a typical case of a gentleman fighting a rogue?)

In late May of 1946, the Nationalist Army counterattacked the Communist Army and took Changchun and pursued the Communist Army to the Songhua River, approaching Harbin. Then, under pressure from Marshall, on June 6 Chiang Kai-shek had to give order to the Nationalist Army to stop further attacks for 15 days. (Another wrong decision.) During the truce, the military trio had talks concerning the restoration of traffic and a truce throughout the northeastern areas. In July, Marshall found that the military conflicts had become worse. In mid-July, seven American marines were kidnapped by the Communist Army in the eastern Hebei province and at the end of July, some American transport trucks were ambushed by the Communist Army on the way from Tianjin to Peking. Three marines were killed and 12 wounded.

At Marshall's suggestion, on the 11th of July, John Leighton Stuart was appointed ambassador in China to help Marshall with the mediations. As Chiang Kai-shek said that the final goal of the Communist Party was to attain power over all the country, not just a truce with the Nationalist government, all these negotiations ended in nothing. On the 15th of November, 1946, the People's Conference for drawing up the constitution opened and the Communist Party refused to attend. On the contrary, they declared on November 16 that they considered the conference unlawful. On January 8, 1947, Marshall went back to America. The Nationalist government was about to send a delegation to YanAn for peace talks, but the Communist Party said that there was no need unless the People's Conference and the Constitution were declared unlawful.

So the door to peace talks was closed.

The Nationalist Government Was Expelled to Taiwan

The second civil war actually began

On the 26th of June, 1946, the day when the effective truce period was over, the Nationalist Army started their onslaught to the Communist Army, but they had already escaped. This date is considered by historians as the actual outbreak of the second civil war between the Communist Party and the Nationalist Party.

To protect the Nanking wing, from July to December, the Nationalist Army attacked the Communist Army in the northern Jiangsu province seven times. The result was that the Nationalist Army occupied all the towns in that area, but the Communist Army annihilated the 69th division of the Nationalist

Army. Who was the winner? The Communist Party. The towns were still there. If they were lost, they could be retaken some time later. But once a division was wiped out, the Nationalist Army had lost a division forever. Mao Zedong's strategy was to make the first aim the annihilation of the Nationalist army, not to keep possession of towns. Once the Nationalist Army was totally wiped out, who could fight them for the towns? Therefore, from a strategic point of view, Chiang Kai-shek and the Nationalist Party were doomed to lose in the long run.

On the 20th of July, the Communist Army began their attack of Datong town in Shanxi province. In August they surrounded the town, but by September they could not take the town and had to retreat. In October, Marshall was hard at work trying to broker an agreement, but the Nationalist government made two last minute demands that again sabotaged his efforts. On October 11, the Nationalist Army made a surprise attack and took Zhangjiakou in Hebei province. When Liang Shuming, a mediator belonging to none of the parties, read in the newspapers that Zhangjiakou was taken by the Nationalist Army, he sighed, "By the time we woke up, the peace was already over."

But he was wrong in that. When Mao secretly made up his mind to rule China by himself with his party, peace was already out of the question. Chiang Kai-shek only wanted to his rule and that of the Nationalist Party to last a bit longer, hoping to defeat the Communist Party by force. However, he always chose wrong tactics, so his case was already hopeless. Wise stratagems can enable the weak to conquer the strong. If statesmen or generals wish to be wise and victorious, they must learn from history.

On August 10, the Communist Army occupied some hundreds of miles of railway line between Tangshan and Lanfeng. When the Nationalist Army counterattacked, the Communist Army withdrew but they annihilated another division of the Nationalist Army during the process, in early September. In late October, the Nationalist Army took 25 towns and it looked like victory was theirs. But they were wrong. The Communist Party still had their full forces while the Nationalist Army was diminishing, division by division. Once they had a town, they had taken on a burden, just like the Japanese army had done. If Chiang Kai-shek had been wise enough, he would have concentrated his army on wiping out the Communist Army bit by bit. Instead he lost the mainland to the Communists. The tragic fate of the common Chinese people was thus sealed.

From December in 1946 to April in 1947, the Communist Army eliminated more than 40,000 of the National troops and took 11 towns in the northeastern provinces. On the 10th of March, 1947, the Nationalist Army came to assail YanAn. The Communist Army withdrew from it and adopted their well-known guerrilla strategies. The Nationalist Army could not get at them, let alone to extinguish them.

In Shandong province, the Communist Party often boasted of their best strategy used in the campaign in Mengliaggu area from late March to early May. The Nationalist Army gathered 450,000 men and planned to occupy all the areas so-called liberated from the Communist Party. The Nationalist Army strategy was to advance step by step, pushing forward like a wall and leaving no gap for guerrilla movements, which was temporarily successful. But the strategy of the Communist Army was to make a sham retreat to let the enemy think that they were trying to escape, while they would seek for chances to attack a small part of the Nationalist Army. Like eating a big cake, bite by bite.

The 74th division of the Nationalist Army was thought of as a trump division, but Zhang Lingfu, their commander, was an arrogant and thoughtless man, though brave. He marched ahead, leaving other two divisions far behind. Although this region was controlled by the Nationalist Army, there were gaps between their troops. So the Communist Army made a bold plan to wedge between the groups and surround the 74th division. When Chiang Kai-shek learned that his 74th division was in danger, he commanded other divisions close to Zhang to rush to his rescue. The Communist Army knew that reinforcements would be coming from the Nationalist Army, as usual, and so they ambushed them at Huangya Mountain and blocked the way to Mengliaggu.

This was the decisive battle. Whoever won in this battle would win in the entire campaign in the region. The Communist Army reached the top of the mountain a few minutes earlier, seizing the high ground, and got control of the entire battlefield. Though the national reinforcements did their best to launch attack after attack from the foot of the mountain, geography was not in their favor. Meanwhile, the Communist Army poured fire at the surrounded 74th division. The Communist Army sent a suicide squad to steal in and make a surprise attack on the command center of the 74th division, which was in a cave. When they got to the entrance, only three of them were still alive. They shouted, "The first battalion go east; the second battalion west; the third battalion, block the front exit." Then they yelled inside, "Hands up!" When Commander Zhang Lingfu came out and saw only three of them, he fired and killed one. But a Communist soldier shot him dead before he could do more. The whole 74th division and a regiment from the 83rd division with them were all eradicated, over 30,000 in all.

On the 31st of July, 1947, the Communist Party officially named their army the Chinese People's Liberation Army (PLA, as it is known today), and it was divided into four so-called field armies. They recruited mostly young people in the countryside, who were generally illiterate and easily tricked into sacrificing their lives. So their army swelled in size. They used ten times the troops to attack the Nationalist Army and it was said that when one enemy soldier was killed, they could sacrifice ten of theirs.

In the second civil war, there were three major campaigns besides many minor battles.

The campaign in the northeastern provinces

The first campaign was waged from the 12th of September to the 2nd of November, in 1948, in the northeastern provinces. There the situation was favorable to the Communist "Liberation" army, because during the Anti-Japanese war, they had guerrillas in the northeastern China controlling wide swathes of the countryside. When the Nationalist Army was transported there to take over what was in the hands of the Japanese army, they only occupied cities such as Shenyang, Changchun and Jinzhou. The Communist Party wanted to take over all the provinces in the northeastern China first, because there were factories that could make weapons for them, and also this area provided grain supplies for their army. Then they would go down south to the coastline.

For this campaign, the 4th field army, under the command of

Lin Biao, gathered 700,000 men while the Nationalist Army had only 550,000. As a result, the casualties of the Liberation Army, including those wounded, were 609,000 and those of the Nationalist Army 470,000.

At the beginning of the campaign, the Communist Liberation Army had already surrounded Changchun. They originally planned that if they could take Changchun, they would get supplies from it. However, the city was built so strong that it was not easy to take. Therefore, they had to surround it lest the Nationalist Army in the city came out to interfere with their other schemes. On the 7th of September, Mao telegrammed Lin Biao to attack Jinzhou. If they occupied Jinzhou area, they would block the Nationalist Army from escaping south.

On the 24th of September, 1948, the Nationalist Army telegrammed Chiang Kai-shek for reinforcements. Chiang commanded Wei Lihuang in Shenyang to send a detachment to rescue the army in Jinzhou, but Wei refused to carry out the order on the excuse that it might jeopardize the safety of Shenyang. Chiang had to transport the 49th army by air to Jinzhou. But only two regiments landed successfully. Then the airport was blocked by Communist anti-aircraft guns on the 28th and the airplanes could not land any more. On October 1, the Communist Liberation Army surrounded Jinzhou after taking over all other towns in its vicinity.

On October 2, Chiang Kai-shek flew to Shenyang to summon a military meeting and decided to send seven divisions from Shandong province by sea to the Hulu Islands, and from there to Jinzhou. Next day he left Shenyang by plane. When Lin Biao learned of Chiang's plan, he accelerated his attack on Jinzhou. If the Tashan line was broken through by the Nationalist reinforcements, the whole campaign would end in failure.

On October 10, the Nationalist reinforcements reached Tashan and the fight started. On October 13, Tashan was still under the control of the Liberation Army. On the 14th, Tashan changed hands nine times, but the Nationalist Army still could not break through the line. While the fighting was severe at Tashan, an attack on Jinzhou began at 10 o'clock that morning. Some 500 cannons fired at targets in the city. At 11:30AM, the communist foot soldiers rushed forth. When the soldiers in the front fell, the soldiers behind took up their positions. The attack lasted till 6:00PM on October 15 when the Liberation Army entered the city. Over 100,000 Nationalist Army fighters were eliminated. The vice commander-in-chief, Fan Hanji, and the commander of the 6th bloc, Lu Junquan, were captured. When the Nationalist reinforcements heard of the fall of Jinzhou, they retreated to the Hulu islands.

There were only two cities left to be conquered: Shenyang and Changchun. The eastern half of Changchun was guarded by the 60th army, under the command of Zeng Zesheng, who was a friend of Lu Junquan. Therefore, Lin Biao ordered Lu Junquan to contact Zeng Zesheng to talk him into betraying Chiang Kai-shek and turning over to the Communist Party. A telegram was sent to Zeng in Lu's name. Seeing the Nationalist Army was in a bad situation, Zeng declared an uprising on October 17, with his three divisions, 26,000 in number. That night, the Liberation Army stealthily took up position in the eastern half of Changchun. On October 19 day, the new 7th army surrendered to the Liberation Army. The commander-in-chief in the city, Zheng Tongguo, contacted the Liberation Army and asked for permission to put up two more days' fake resistance before he surrendered. After he surrendered, a false news bulletin should then be issued that he was captured. Thus Changchun city fell into the possession of the Liberation Army. On October 31st, the Liberation Army surrounded the last city, Shenyang, and at dawn November 1, the attack on the city commenced. After one day's fight, the Communist Liberation Army occupied the city. All the northeastern provinces were under the control of the Communist Party.

The campaign in Huaihai River area

The Huaihai River campaign took place between the 6th of November in 1948 and the 10th of January in 1949. The Liberation Army threw in 600,000 men and the Nationalist Army had 800,000. The casualties, including wounded, of the Liberation Army were over 100,000 while those of the Nationalist Army, including those captured, were as high as 550,000.

The defense minister of the Nationalist Party was convinced that if they wanted to control the Yangtze River defensive line, they must control the Huaihai River defensive line. Obviously, the war in the Huaihai River area was very important to the Nationalist government. While the campaign in the northeastern provinces were still going on, a battle in JiNan city was engaged. The Liberation Army used 140,000 soldiers to attack the city and 180,000 to block the reinforcements from Xuzhou city. At that time, the Nationalist Army in Xuzhou area should have gone to the rescue of the army in JiNan. But the Liberation Army blocked their way. They hesitated to advance.

After the Liberation Army took JiNan on the 24th of September, 1948, they marched towards Xuzhou. The Nationalist Army gathered in Xuzhou area for the defense. On the night of the 6th of November, the Liberation Army officially began its campaign in the Huaihai River area. When they found that the national 7th military bloc was receding, they pursued and caught the 7th bloc on the 7th day while the bloc was crossing the Great Canal.

The 63rd army and the 83rd division, bringing up the rear, were quickly wiped out. When the commander of the 7th bloc called the commander of the 13th bloc, the latter refused to come to his assistance, saying that he had to adhere to the original plan to retreat. (That was one of the reasons why the Nationalist Army was eaten up bit by bit. No cooperation between commanders. They could not form a fist to strike at the foe, only using fingers separately to tear at it.) On the 8th of November, three fourths of the Nationalist Army defending the river line held an uprising under the instructions of the Communist Party members who were lurking within the army. Therefore, the Liberation Army cut through the line easily.

Having crossed the Great River, the Nationalist 7th bloc decided to stay at Zhanzhuang and to fight the pursuing Liberation Army. Anyway, more liberation forces came and surrounded the 7th bloc on November 11. Chiang Kai-shek ordered the 13th bloc and the 2nd bloc to rescue the 7th bloc, and moreover, sent the 6th bloc and the 8th bloc to the Xuzhou area. The forces of the Nationalist Army increased to 800,000. On November 13, the reinforcements of the 2nd and 13th blocs came to the Daxujia line, and were stopped there by the Liberation 3rd field army. Since the reinforcements of the Nationalist Army got through the blockading line, the Liberation Army quickened its attack and annihilated the 7th bloc on November 22.

On the 30th of November, 300,000 defensive Nationalist Army under the command of Du Yuming left Xuzhou and went south. A 300,000-man detachment of the Liberation Army chased them. At the time, Chiang Kai-shek ordered Du to go southeast to rescue the 12th bloc, the 2nd bloc, the 13th bloc and the 16th bloc, separately surrounded in the region northeast to Yong town. But on the 4th of December, the 16th bloc acted on its own, trying to break through the encirclement, and was eliminated. On December 12, the Liberation Army pounced on the 12th bloc and wiped it out on the December 15.

Then the Liberation Army aimed at Du Yuming and asked him to surrender, but Du refused, even though he was already surrounded. Two more blocs were annihilated on the 9th of January in 1949, and Du was taken captive on the 10th. The 6th and 8th blocs deserted their defensive posts between the Huaihai River and the Yangtze River and retreated to the south of the Yangtze River. The vast expanse of land to the north of the Yangtze River fell into the hands of the Liberation Army. Thus ended the campaign in the Huaihai River area.

The campaign in Peking and Tianjin area

This campaign lasted for 64 days, from the 29th of November, 1948 to the 31st of January, 1949. The Liberation Army threw 1,000,000 troops into that campaign and the Nationalist Army gathered over 500,000. The Liberation Army had 39,000 casualties (including the wounded) while the Nationalist Army lost 52,000 (including captured).

When the liberation 4th field army occupied the northeastern provinces, they marched south to attack Peking and Tianjin. General Fu Zuoyi (1895–1974) was the commander of the defense of Peking. Before the campaign started, Chiang Kai-shek wanted Fu to bring his army south to strengthen the defensive line by the Yangtze River. But Fu did not follow Chiang's orders. Fu planned to keep only Peking and Tianjin area in his control and give up the other towns. If the situation became critical, he could escape by sea and get south of the Yangtze River.

The Liberation Army's strategy was to surround each of the cities and towns separately to prevent anyone from escaping.

They saw Peking as the center of this area and attacked towns along the outermost circle, and closing in their encirclement towards the center. In late December, they took over two towns in the west. On the 14th of January, 1949, they besieged Tianjin city when the defensive army refused to surrender. After fighting for 29 hours, they entered the city, eliminating 10 divisions, 160,000 soldiers (including captured).

At last they came to Peking. They did not want any damage done to the old capital city, and they therefore sent someone to talk to Fu Zuoyi. Seeing that escape was out of the question, he declared an uprising and went over to the Liberation Army. Later, in the second republic of China, he was appointed the Minister of Water Resources.

The end of the second civil war

As the situation became more dire for the Nationalist government, Chiang Kai-shek resigned, leaving everything in the hands of the vice president Li Zongren (1891–1969), who proposed starting peace talks with the Communist Party. Meanwhile, Chiang transferred 4.5 million taels of gold and $384 million to Taiwan (the island of Formosa). At the beginning of 1949, the Nationalist government had already moved its capital from Nanking to Canton. On April 1, 1949, the representatives of both the Communist Party and the Nationalist Party had peace talks in Peking. The Communist Party wanted the Nationalist Party to accept conditions that amounted to a complete surrender. of course, the Nationalist government spurned such a suggestion.

On the night of the 21st of April, the combined Liberation Army of the 2nd and 3rd field armies crossed the Yangtze River in wooden sailboats in the face of artillery fire from the National army along the river. They broke through the weak spots of the defensive line and set foot on the south bank of the river. The 35th army, belonging to the 8th bloc of the 3rd field army, were tasked with attacking Nanking. On the night of the 23rd, they crossed the river and reached Nanking. All the important members of the Nationalist government had already left the city by air. So on April 24, the Liberation Army entered the city as if it was entirely undefended. Afterwards, the Communist government decided that the 23rd of April should be the anniversary of the liberation of Nanking, though formally they took over the city on the 24th.

The Liberation Army took over Hangzhou on May 3, and Hankou on May 18, and Wuchang and Hanyang on May 17. They took Nanchang on May 22. At the same time, on May 12, the Liberation Army began to attack Shanghai. They first laid siege to the satellite towns around Shanghai and met strong resistance. Anyway, they took them one by one, and on May 26, they entered the urban area of Shanghai. The next day, all of Shanghai was controlled by the Liberation Army. People in Shanghai welcomed the Liberation Army just as they had welcomed Chiang Kai-shek's army after the long occupation by Japan. But they had been disappointed by the corruption in Chiang Kai-shek's government. So now they pinned their hopes on the Communist Party, not knowing at that time whether the Communist Party would disappoint them just the same.

On April 24, the Liberation Army took Taiyuan, the capital of Shanxi province, and took XiAn, the capital of Shaanxi province on May 20. They stormed into Qingdao, a harbor city in Shandong province, on June 2. On August 4, Cheng Quan, chairman of Hunan province and Chen Mingren, commander of the 1st bloc there, declared he was betraying the Nationalist government and went over to the Liberation Army, and so the capital Changsha changed hands peacefully. The Liberation Army occupied Lanzhou, the capital of Gansu province, on August 26, and then Fuzhou, the capital of Fujian province, and then Canton on October 14. The Nationalist government had already packed up and moved to Zhongqing again. On October 17 they took Amoy but failed in the attempt to take Quemoy on the 25th and the Zhoushan islands on the 3rd of November.

In November, Chiang Kai-shek flew to Chongqing and on November 20, Li Zongren went to Hong Kong. On November 15, the Liberation Army took Guiyang, the capital of Guizhou province, and Chongqing on November 30 when the Nationalist government had already moved to Chengdu. On the 7th of December, the Nationalist government declared it was moving its capital offshore to Taipei in Taiwan. So from December 8 to 10, all the VIPs of the government were flying to Taipei. On December 9, the chairmen of Yunnan province and of Xikang province declared they were siding with the Liberation Army, which entered these provinces without any hitch. On December 27, they took Chengdu, the capital of Sichuan province. The next spring, on March 27, 1950, they took Xichang. By then, almost the whole country was under the control of the Communist Party.

PART TWO

THE SECOND REPUBLIC—

THE PEOPLE'S REPUBLIC OF CHINA

CHAPTER 5. THE ESTABLISHMENT OF THE PEOPLE'S REPUBLIC OF CHINA

The Chinese People's Political Consultative Conference

When the Communist Liberation Army was still fighting the Nationalist Army, the Communist Party summoned the Chinese people's political consultative conference from the 21st to 30th of September, 1949. A few so-called democratic parties attended the conference, such as the Revolutionary Committee of the Nationalist Party (part of the Nationalist Party that favored the Communist Party), Chinese Democratic League, China Democratic National Construction Association, China Association for Promoting Democracy, Chinese Peasants and Workers Democratic Party, China Zhigong Party, and Jiusan Society, eight in all. These so-called democratic parties have been give the ironic label of "vases" as they were nothing but empty vessels to decorate the political Communist Party conferences as symbols of democracy, because they have no say in whatever national affairs. They can only say yes to whatever the Communist Party says, and if there is a vote, every one of them will put up their hands to make up a 100% positive vote so that the Communist Party can boast of having full support. A standing committee was formed to handle routine matters. The chairman, vice chairmen, and the chief secretary controlled everything. But the chairman had to be a top-ranking Communist Party member.

In this conference a so-called Common Program was passed as the temporary constitution, which was composed of 7 chapters and 60 articles. The Common Program outlined the state system and the system of the government as the "democracy and dictatorship of the Chinese people" (meaning democracy to the people and dictatorship to the enemy) who consisted of the proletariat (workers), peasantry, petty bourgeoisie, national bourgeoisie, and other democratic patriots. (The Communist Party divides the bourgeoisie in China into two types: national capitalists and bureaucratic capitalists.) It was a united front with the proletariat in the leadership (through the Communist Party) on the basis of the alliance of workers and peasants. The government would confiscate all the private properties of the bureaucratic capitalists, which denoted only Chiang Kai-shek, Tse-ven Soong (Chiang's brother-in-law, who was the head of the executive office, equivalent to the Cabinet), Kung Hsiang-His (simplified as H. H. Kung, and jokingly called Ha-Ha- Kung, who married the sister of Chiang Kai-shek's wife and was the financial minister most of the time), and the Chen brothers, Chen Guofu (the minister of the central organization ministry of the Nationalist Party) and Chen Lifu (education minister). Their father was the sworn brother of Chiang Kai-shek. All other private business owners were defined as national capitalists.

The major articles of the Common Program—the temporary constitution—stated that citizens of the Peoples' Republic of China had the rights of voting and nomination, but actually none but the leaders of the Communist Party had the rights to nominate candidates. They could nominate whomever they liked and even themselves. As for voting rights, common voters could not vote for whomever they preferred, but were forced to vote for those on the list made by the party leaders. If there were ten candidates, a voter could not vote for fewer than ten. He or she had to make a mark next to every name on the list, or he or she would get in trouble. Once a young worker crossed out a name on the list and added the name of his boss. Although he was also a party member, he was severely criticized not following the rules.

Another major article asserted that the people of the republic were to enjoy freedom of thought, speech, gathering, organizing societies, communication, personal liberty, living anywhere, moving anywhere, religions and beliefs, and to demonstrate. But all these rights existed only on paper. In reality, no one could exercise such rights. Everything going on under the sun, or even at night, was monitored by the Communist Party.

The Ceremony of the Establishment of the People's Republic of China

At 2:00PM on the 1st of October, 1949, the committee of the central people's government had its first session and selected Mao Zedong as chairman. Zhu De, Liu Shaoqi, Soong Ching-ling, Li Jishen, Zhang Lan, and Gao Gang became the vice chairmen, Zhou Enlai was the Premier of the state council and the foreign minister as well, and Zhu De was the commander-in-chief of the Chinese People's Liberation Army. At 3:00, a ceremony marking the establishment of the People's Republic of China was held at TianAnMen (literally Gate of Heavenly Peace). Chairman Mao announced the formation of the People's Republic of China. On December 2, the central people's government approved the decision to make October 1 the national day every year.

Accordingly, on the 1st of October, 1950, the leaders of the Communist Party were expected to stand at TianAnMen to watch the parade going through TianAnMen Square. A plot was revealed to murder the leaders. Two tenants had moved into a house at No. 17 in the Ganyu Alley northeast of TianAnMen, two mercenary spies, one Italian and the other Japanese. One night in February 1950, two strangers came to see the Japanese man, who had an 82 mortar. In mid-September, the Chinese police department intercepted a letter mailed to Tokyo, Japan, in which there was a sketch of the clear outline of TianAnMen with two black arrows, one pointing to the top of the gate and the other pointing to tiny figures drawn on the square. The letter described the layout of TianAnMan Square. Through analysis, Beijing police declared that it was evidence of a serious scheme to murder the government leaders. After further investigations, at dawn on September 27, the police rushed to the No. 17 house and broke in. They took the Japanese and Italian spies into custody. In the

Japanese man's room they found letters, documents, diagrams, the 82 mortar, and a pistol with 235 bullets, and found in the Italian's room a packet of poisonous powder, a diagram with the outline of TianAnMen and a parabola pointing to it. On October 10, the Central Committee of the Communist Party (not the central government) issued an instruction to round up and arrest reactionaries, including spies. Who would be considered a reactionary? Those executing the instruction would define it at will.

The Ruling System of the People's Republic of China

There are two vertical hierarchies in the ruling system under the Communist Party. One is the formal government line and the other is the party line. On the same level, there are party organizations as well as government departments. Let's take Shanghai for an example. On the municipal level, the mayor is the head of the Shanghai government, but there is also the party secretary of the Shanghai municipal committee. The mayor must obey the party secretary, which means that the party secretary is the real head of the city, the over-lord. For every department or bureau in the municipal government, there is also a party organization on the same level.

Urban Shanghai is divided into 10 precincts with the same two-dimensional ruling system at every level. Under the precinct level are street committees, under which are resident committees which are the basic ruling cells. Every resident committee comprises the residents in one block. All cadres of these committees at different levels are paid by the government. Then every block is divided into several groups. The group leaders, though appointed, get no pay from the government. They are either housewives or retired people, always around. The group leaders must report to the resident committee what happens in the block and if they suspect any resident of anything unusual, they must report on that. The head of the resident committee is called director and there is also a party secretary.

The municipal police station also has a party secretary. On the precinct level, there is a precinct station under which there are several police branches at the same level with the street committees. Every police branch will assign a policeman to work with the resident committee and the resident committee cadres obey the policeman.

In the suburbs of Shanghai there are 10 counties. Every county ruled over several villages, which were called communes in the period from the Great Leap Forward to the end of the Great Cultural Revolution. Under the commune level there are productive teams. All peasants belong to different teams. Peasants and city residents are all tied to where they live and are not generally free to relocate. All their behavior and actions will be reported to the party at different levels. People may work in companies of all sorts, or in stores and schools, belonging to the government. They are told to watch over each other's behavior and actions and report to the party if anything is suspicious. Everyone takes it seriously, because if one reports some colleague's misbehavior, he is deemed loyal to the party and will receive some compensation such as a promotion, a small raise, or even be allowed to join the party—the fastest way to become an official. Even relatives and family members will report on their near ones for their own benefits. Under this sort of system one feels that there are spies all around. That is how the Chinese people lived until Deng Xiaoping's 1978 economic reform and "opening up" policy. (Of course not everyone liked that either: Under this sort of system, it seems that everything is suddenly open, like prostitution, embezzlement and corruption.)

CHAPTER 6. THE MASSACRE OF REACTIONARIES AND THE SUPPRESSION OF BANDITS

The Movement to Arrest and Kill Reactionaries

The action against "reactionaries" began in December 1950 and went on until October 1951. It involved 3 million people. So lots of innocent people were arrested and many of them were executed. At that time, people were easily executed without proper legal procedures. A person could be killed just on the word of a work team leader. Fan Yuanmao, a communist activist, told of his experience at that time. He had been a district government leader and presided over many public judgments, that is, meetings to decide how many people and which ones should be executed. At one of such meeting, twelve people would be shot to death. A few more people were also named, who were called "to accompany those going to die," but in fact they were sent there to watch the twelve people being shot, which served as a lesson to others not to do anything against the Party. At Fan Yuanmao's order, those persons were dragged out into an open field to be executed just as pigs are dragged into a slaughter house. One of the few watchers was mistakenly killed. When asked what to do about the error, Fan answered that he would just hand in another form with the name of that person to bring the number of those executed up to thirteen. Easily settled. No other procedures needed. The lives of common Chinese people weigh no more than a feather, as a Chinese saying goes.

In some places, father and son, brothers, cousins, were killed together, maybe the whole family executed, just like in the feudal age under the rule of the emperors. One "funny" story says that the names of those who were to be executed were written in a booklet, which would be given to a cadre of higher rank for final approval. That guy would stamp a seal on each page that meant that the death decision was final. After the guy stamped a few pages, he stood up to get a glass of water. Then a gust of wind blew in and turned two pages over. When the guy came back to sit at his desk, he continued to stamp the pages till the last page. So the couple of people whose names were on the pages without a stamp were not executed. The gust of wind saved them. All in all, years later, the Party admitted that many innocent people were mistakenly executed. They died for nothing. Victims of the Party and Mao's overly drastic actions.

It has been argued that in so many dynasties in the history of China, and elsewhere, many innocent people have been mistakenly killed. It's difficult to make comparisons. But it is totally wrong to kill innocent people and it does not matter how many or how few are killed. According to the Communist Party, all the dynasties in history were a form of feudalism, a bad political system. That innocent people were killed in a bad system may be no surprise. But the Communist Party of China boasted that socialism is the best political system in the world and claimed from the beginning that the Party was serving the people. Apparently, a hypothetical system is one thing and the individuals who seek to establish and implement it may be a different story altogether.

Some ridiculous things happened during this movement. In February of 1951, Mao summoned a meeting to decide the rate at which people should be executed. They decided that the rate should be one in a thousand, and at first, half of this number should be killed, and then the policy should be reviewed. Mao gave clear instructions to the mayors of Shanghai and Nanking, saying, "Shanghai is a large city of 6 million, and in Shanghai hardly more than 200 are executed out of over 20,000 arrested. It is not enough. In my opinion, at least 3,000 or so should be executed. Nanking was the capital of the Nationalist Party; the reactionaries there should be executed and I don't mean a few more than 200. Far more must be executed in Nanking." Mao's decision to kill people was not based on crimes those people committed but based on his own whim.

On the 21st of February, 1950, the state council issued the "Rules for punishing reactionaries in the People's Republic of China." Here reactionaries were defined as: people contacting imperialists; contacting, instigating and bribing officials, armed forces and militia to commit treason; gathering armed crowds for rebellion; joining spy organizations; organizing or utilizing any religious groups for reactionary purposes; robbing or damaging public or private property or public equipment; using poison to kill people; making fake documents or IDs; instigating crowds against the government; sowing discord among government officials; spreading rumors; stealing across territory borders; breaking into or escaping from jails; hiding or protecting reactionaries, etc. It didn't matter if the action had been completed or not.

Even those Party members who had worked as communist spies in the former government were deemed traitors and killed; let alone those generals who had changed sides from Chiang Kai-shek's government to the Communist Party. They were also killed. In some people's opinion, those generals, if they saw no hope of winning the day, should have gone abroad to live a free, safe life, not change sides to the Communist Party to be killed later. They should have known that the Communist Party had killed their own comrades even while they were still at YanAn. Those comrades believed in communism and went there to help wage the revolution. They could never dream that they would die in the hands of their own comrades in the name of revolution. Talk about betrayal.

Then there was the "Revolt of Restitution Party." It involved over 1,300 persons, including 80 Communist Party members, in PuEr town in Yunnan Province. PuEr is famous for its PuEr tea. Even the town's party secretary and the deputy director-general of the police station were included. The first party secretary of the province said that he did not believe it. The party organization itself could not get so many members in such a short time— how could a reactionary organization achieve it? Then it was found that the case was made up. No evidence at all, except for one sign calling for revolt, which was drawn by a primary school teacher under threat. So the ridiculous case was dismissed.

In January of 1954, Xu Zirong, the vice minister of the police department, reported the statistics. In this movement, over 2,620,000 people were apprehended, "over 712,000 were executed, over 1,290,000 were imprisoned, and over 1,200,000 were placed under police control. Over 380,000 were released because their crimes were not serious." If 712,000 were executed, the ratio was 0.124% as the population at that time was 500 million.

The Suppression of Bandits

There were two types of bandits operating at this time. One was the kind who had already been bandits during the civil war owing to the chaotic situation. Many of them were common people who had had no other way to survive. The other were former soldiers of the Nationalist Army who had escaped from the People's Liberation Army to dwell in the mountains. They acted as guerrilla warriors for the Nationalist Party, but were deemed bandits by the Liberation Army. Most of those bandits hid in the mountainous southwestern regions, but some lived in towns.

Bandits in Western Hunan

When most of Hunan province fell to the Communists, some of those men still loyal to the Nationalist Army settled in Western Hunan and formed three groups called the Anti-Communist Army, over 100,000 in all. From October 14 to 16, 1949, the 47th Liberation army besieged Dayong and annihilated their 122nd army (4,333 men) and incorporated 12,000 into the Liberation army. This battle frightened other bandits. Some of them decided they'd better go ahead and join the Liberation army. But when the Liberation Army marched towards the southwest, they no longer wanted to surrender. On the contrary, in mid-December, they went to take back Dayong. Some of these bandits attacked a squad of the Liberation army and killed some local armed personnel and pillaged 20 trucks belonging to the army.

To deal with the deteriorating situation, the 47th Liberation army returned to the Western Hunan province and occupied 8 towns. The bandits escaped to some caves in the mountain. The

Liberation Army found the family members of the bandits and made them go into the mountains to ask their husbands to come down and surrender. Finally the Liberation Army attacked the caves and eliminated the rest of the bandits in October.

Bandits in the southwestern provinces

There were 148 groups of bandits in Yunnan province, 541 groups in Guizhou province, and 300 groups in Sichuan province. The big groups had a few thousand men. In February 1950, the bandits in all those areas grew from 400,000 to 500,000.

To annihilate them, the Communist Party sent the 3rd corps, the 4th corps, the 5th corps, and the 18th corps, plus the 7th army to separately attack the bandits in different districts. The attacks began in March 1950. During one month, the Liberation Army wiped out several groups of bandits numbering 23,000 in southern Sichuan province. By the end of July, 950,000 were eliminated in the eastern Sichuan province. After September, the Liberation Army in the eastern Sichuan province maneuvered to the region in the northeastern Guizhou province and annihilated another 320,000 bandits there. By the end of 1950, over 193,000 bandits were eliminated in the eastern Sichuan province, over 293,000 in the southern Sichuan province, over 83,000 in the western Sichuan province, and over 80,000 in the northern Sichuan province. It was reported that by 1953, more than 1,160,000 bandits in the northwestern provinces were wiped out, and over 700 cannons and over 600,000 firearms of all kinds were captured. During the whole process, the bandits assassinated 157 Liberation Army men and local cadres, spread poison 223 times, and set 316 fires. In 1952, the bandits received 10 airdrops including 13 radio sets, and 14 trained spies were sent from Taiwan and landed in those areas.

Bandits in the western Guangxi province

The bandits gathered more than 90,000 men, spreading over 97 towns out of 102 towns in western Guangxi. They killed more than 500 cadres, took away more than 28,000,000 catties of grain (17 tons) and more than 260,000 livestock. They hid in Dayao Mountain. The Liberation Army gathered 14 regiments plus militiamen from 18 towns, and blockaded all the waterways and roads to outside. The bandits tried to break through and escaped more than 40 times, but in the end it all failed. On the 8th of January, 1951, the Liberation Army started into the Dayao Mountain and wiped out more than 400 men in mountain villages. But the bandits were spread throughout the mountains, and so on the 2nd of February, the Communist Party gathered 13 battalions to go village by village and cave by cave searching for them. This campaign went on for 50 days and no more bandits were left in that area. The ringleaders were all executed.

A special case

A weird thing happened one evening in 1950. Near Wulong town in the southeastern Sichuan province, there was a restaurant called Danxin Restaurant which was famous for steamed buns stuffed with ground meat. But what kind of meat it was, no one knew. Someone suspected that it was the human flesh. In the olden days, there were always stories about steamed buns stuffed with human flesh sold in "black inns." This small restaurant was a meeting place for bandits in this area. The owner of the restaurant was an old man with a fake hunchback: the real owner had a hunchback, but he had murdered him. He took over the restaurant and brought in two of his men, disguised as waiters.

On the 21st of October, ten Liberation Army soldiers passed the restaurant. They were on their way back from the mountain fighting bandits. As they were tired and hungry, they went into the restaurant. They were served steamed buns. A young soldier observed that the meat stuffing didn't taste like pork, or mutton or beef. So he asked the owner what meat it was. The owner turned to leave without answering the question. Soon the soldiers were drugged, lying on the floor, and were dragged to the basement.

At daybreak on October 23, another five liberation soldiers came into the restaurant and were also served the steamed buns. Soon they all lay on the floor and were put into the basement. Next, more than 100 soldiers came, but this time they entered the restaurant without asking for any food. They had learned that this restaurant was a hideout and meeting place for bandits and had come to arrest those working here. The basement was found and 5 newcomers were still lying on the ground; two of the former ten soldiers were still alive. The other eight soldiers had been killed. One of the two was the squad leader and he told the story. He went on to live his life; but the other, a younger soldier, went mad and was put into an asylum. He died in March of 1959.

CHAPTER 7. COMMUNIST RULE IN TIBET

The Early Relationship Between Tibet and China

The Tibetan people and the Han Chinese had relations going back to the Tang Dynasty (AD 618–907). In the year of 640, when the famous emperor Tang Taizong was on the throne, Srongtsen Gampo, the sovereign of Tibet at that time, sent his Premier to the Tang capital, bringing 5,000 taels of gold and hundreds of different treasures as gifts and asked for permission to marry a princess. The Tang emperor was pleased and granted the marriage request. Legend had it that the chieftains of other tribes also wanted to marry the princess. The emperor wanted to test the wisdom of all the emissaries and gave them a riddle to see who could solve it. He gave them a thin silk thread and a piece of jade with a hole in the middle, but the hole was zigzag, not straight through. Whoever could get the thread through the hole, his sovereign could marry the princess. None could do it except the Premier from Tibet. He got an ant and tied the thread on the ant. He blew his breath at the ant and it went through the winding hole, carrying the thread through. Therefore, Princess Wencheng (625–680) was sent to Tibet and married the Tibetan sovereign.

The princess brought Tibetans the endowments of Chinese culture, including the silkworm, seeds of bountiful grain, medicine and medical equipment. The sovereign built the Potala Palace in Lhasa for her, in imitation of the style of the Tang palace. In the year 740, another princess of the Tang dynasty married the great grandson of Srongtsen Gampo. At that time, Tibet was an independent nation and did not belong to China. It was, at most, deemed a subordinate state to the Tang Dynasty, but only in name. Not part of China.

At the beginning of the Qing Dynasty (the last dynasty), the Qing army once conquered Tibet. But with the fall of the Qing dynasty, Tibet declared its independence in 1913 and this was recognized internationally at the time. When the Nationalist government was established, Chiang Kai-shek sent envoys twice, but he did not take any military action to subordinate Tibet under his rule.

The Communist Party Conquers Tibet

However, the Communist Army defeated the Tibetan army on October 6, 1950, and they had to surrender. So under orders from Beijing, Tibet had to send a delegation there. On May 23, 1951, the Communist government forced Tibet to sign the "Seventeen Point Agreement for the Peaceful Liberation of Tibet." In the agreement, the Communist Party promised autonomy in Tibet, and freedom of religion, but when the Communist Army entered Tibet they went back on their promise. They never gave Tibet autonomy, and interfered with their spiritual customs. (It might be said, too, that they had promised the Chinese people a united government, democracy, and freedom of speech, which are still written in their constitution.)

In 1959 when Mao was pushing his reforms on the country at large, he wanted to conduct some reforms in Tibet, too. As a result, from March 10 to 20, 1959, some 100,000 Tibetans followed the Dalai Lama south over Mt. Himalaya and escaped into northern India. Then the Communist Party began to tighten its control over the Tibetans.

The history of China contains many examples showing how to maintain a peaceful relationship with minority populations. Even the feudal rulers, that is, emperors, knew that if they conquered them by force, they would not obey peacefully.

CHAPTER 8. THE LAND REFORM MOVEMENT AND PROSTITUTION REFORM

The Land Reform in the Countryside

As early as 1946, the Communist Party had carried out some reform policies in the districts under their control. On October 10, 1947, they issued new land laws to distribute the arable land to those who actually tilled it. They expropriated the landowners and gave the land to the peasants, thus winning much gratitude and support from the rural populace. This support took two forms: grain and army recruits. Since most of the population in China was in the countryside, when the forces of the Nationalist Party diminished, the Communist Party gained reinforcements by recruiting young peasants.

From winter of 1950 to spring of 1953, the land reform movement began in full swing in all the newly controlled provinces. They divided the arable land belonging to landowners among peasants. On June 30, 1950, the central people's government issued the "Land Reform Law of the People's Republic of China."

Many Party cadres formed work teams and went to the countryside to instruct peasants on how to proceed. The landowners were pulled out of their residences and taken to an open space. They were forced to kneel for long periods on the hard ground.

Those peasants who hated their landowners went forward to slap their faces, and they slapped hard. But the humiliation and sense of injustice were worse than the physical pain. Many of the landowners were shot to death. Their families were deprived of their property, leaving them only with the bare necessities of life. Peasants moved into the landowners' houses.

Fate is full of irony. One tale says that a young man, the son of a landlord, inherited a large stretch of land upon his father's death, and so he became a landlord. He loved to gamble and in the end lost all he owned on the gaming table. He became a poor man. When the Communist Party came and the land reform movement began, he was safe—no one beat him, as he was no longer a member of the ownership class. But the man who had won all his land was deemed a landlord and was killed. Very funny. Or is it?

Statistics showed that out of 2,742 villages in the south of Jiangsu province, beatings happened in 200 villages, and 218 individual landowners were beaten, left hanging up, forced to kneel, and stripped of their clothes. In Henan province, over forty landowners were killed in one month. In Guangdong province, at first the movement went slowly and peacefully. Then Mao learned that not much was happening, and he was dissatisfied. In February 1952, Mao instructed them to pick up the pace. So a slogan went round in that province: "Every village must have blood running. Every landowning family must have beating." As a result, in the western part of that province 1,156 persons committed suicide or were beaten to death.

At the beginning of the movement, some Party leaders had proposed peaceful reform, but Mao persisted in violent reforms. His fundamental theory was based on class conflict. But he treasured his own life. Legend says that in his early revolutionary life, he was once caught by a soldier while he was making an escape. The soldier did not really know who he was. Mao bribed him, and so he let Mao go.

Prostitution Reform in Cities

Prostitution was an old business in almost every nation in the world. Prostitution in China had a history of 3,000 years in written records, and it was generally practiced in cities. Most prostitutes were forced to be in this business; some had even been kidnapped and sold to the whorehouse. Occasionally little girls were sold to the whorehouse by poor parents on the verge of starvation. The parents reasoned that at least their daughter would not starve to death that way. Therefore, girls who were prostitutes were not considered blameworthy for their own sake. (In today's China, the importance of money has increased and it is true that most who become prostitutes do it of their own accord. There are cafes and clubs where a man can pay a young and pretty girl to keep him company while sipping tea, coffee or other drinks, or to dance, and he can invite the girl for more. These girls were called 'Miss.' So nowadays, if anyone calls a girl 'Miss,' she will find it insulting.)

At the beginning of the People's Republic of China, the Communist Party wanted to end the prostitution business once for all. So every local government closed all the whorehouses in their cities, starting with Beijing. The mayor simply declared, at 5 o'clock in the afternoon on the 21st of November in 1949, a ban on the prostitution business and closed all the whorehouses. The chief of the main police station in Beijing gave orders to gather 2,400 cadres and policemen to form 27 groups. At 8:00PM, every group went to the designated district, and 224 whorehouses were closed and 1,316 prostitutes were penned up in penitentiaries for half a year. After "re-education" and healing and a skills-training process, about 400 of them married workers and shop assistants to start their new life. Around 200 of them married peasants in the suburbs of Beijing. Another 200 became workers themselves in textile factories. It is said that 379 returned to their respective homes, while 62 were assigned jobs in theaters or hospitals.

On November 23, Shanghai followed suit and began to close all the whorehouses. In Shanghai 7,400 prostitutes were sent to penitentiaries and turned over a new leaf. During 1951 and 1952, all other cities did the same and prostitution was cleared up in China. As there were so many women who had to build a new life, some of them were sent to join the so-called construction army in the very remote northwest, the Xinjiang Autonomous Region. In April of 1955, 920 girls started from Shanghai, in new green uniforms, and rode a train to barracks there.

Besides the prostitution problem, another problem in the cities was the great number of beggars, homeless and thieves. They were also rounded up by the local police and put in penitentiaries. Then after skills-training, they got jobs, too. During these years, passengers in trams and buses had no fear of pickpockets. Even housewives, if any needed to work to earn money, could be assigned jobs in some kind of factory or low-paying "productive group." Jobs in the productive groups including sealing envelopes, making match boxes, or knitting work, etc. Jobs were not searched out and applied for, but allotted by the local government.

CHAPTER 9. THE KOREAN WAR

North Korea Invaded South Korea

A legend about Korea and China goes back to the end of the Shang Dynasty (1765–1122 BC). The last king of that dynasty was a tyrant and often killed innocent people, even his courtiers. When he was overthrown by the Zhou Dynasty (1121–476 BC), he burned himself to death. His brother Jizi escaped to Korea with his followers, bringing Chinese culture, etiquette and government systems there. The natives supported him to be the first king of Korea. It was called Jizi Korea, which lasted from 1122 BC to 194 BC.

The Korean War, or Korean Conflict, began on June 25, 1950, when the North Korean army marched across the line of demarcation, the 38th parallel, and suddenly attacked the 17th Regiment of the South Korean army without any warning. The war ended on July 27, 1953, when the cease-fire agreement was signed.

The Soviet Union was behind North Korea in waging the war, helped by China. Before the war, the leader of North Korea asked China to send over three divisions composed entirely of Koreans. These became the 4th field army under Lin Biao. The three divisions doubled the military forces of North Korea. Then North Korea concentrated great numbers of tanks and troops to press the South Korean army southward. Meanwhile North Korean troops made an amphibious landing at Kangnung on the east coast right on the south side of the 38th parallel. Then North Korean fighter aircraft attacked Seoul and Kimpo Airfield, destroying a US Air Force C-54 on the ground on Kimpo Airfield. Therefore, John Muccio, the US Ambassador to South Korea, conveyed to US President Truman the request of South Korean government for air assistance and ammunition.

The United Nations Security Council held an emergency meeting, which the representative of the Soviet Union did not attend. The United Nations Security Council called in unison for an immediate cease-fire and withdrawal of the North Korean army to the north of the 38th parallel and authorized the United Nations members to aid South Korea. The United Nations Security Council requested that the US government establish a United Nations Command under an American officer. General MacArthur was appointed as commander of the United Nations army, and he ordered the US Air Force to attack the North Korean units in the south of the 38th parallel.

The US government began the air evacuation of its citizens from South Korea. The next day, the North Korean army occupied Chunchon, Pochon, and Tongduchon in South Korea. So the US 7th fleet sailed north from the Philippines. The US Air Force started to attack the North Korean army, but failed to prevent it from advancing. Soon the North Korean army captured Seoul, the capital of South Korea, overran the port of Inchon, seized the airfield at Kimpo, and threatened the city of Suwon. Then President Truman ordered some units of US navy to approach the Korean peninsula for the purpose of blockading the North Korea army.

At the end of July, as the North Korean troops kept advancing, the United Nations forces had to retreat to a new defensive line along the Naktong River. Then the United States troops launched their first ground offensive, marching from Masan westward toward Chinju to stabilize the southwestern end of the Pusan line. A few days later, US troops, with the aid of air strikes, drove the North Korean army at the Yongsan bridgehead back across the Naktong River.

September was the turning point. At the beginning, the

North Korean army almost reached the brink of total victory, but at the end of the month it was in full withdrawal to the north side of the 38ᵗʰ parallel. The North Korean army's week-long offensive did not succeed in driving the forces of United Nations and South Korea into the sea. By mid-September when the Eighth Army was ready to attack, the United Nations forces found that they were facing a North Korean army that was out of ammunition and other necessary supplies. Simultaneously, General MacArthur launched an amphibious attack at Inchon. The attackers drove a wedge between the North Korean army in the south and its chief supply routes in the north, intending to press the North Korean army against the Eighth Army marching from the southeast. So the North Korean army had to beat a quick retreat northward.

Close to the end of the month, US troops from Inchon and Pusan joined each other near Osan. The United Nations army took 125,000 North Korean soldiers prisoners of war. The South Korean government was now back in Seoul. And the United Nations and South Korean forces reached the 38ᵗʰ parallel.

The Joint Chiefs of Staff commanded General MacArthur to wipe out the North Korean army once and for all so that there would be no further conflict. To do so, they would have to march across the 38ᵗʰ parallel into North Korea. Only the South Korean army was allowed to do that. So for the first time the South Korean troops marched into North Korea. Toward the end of October, the South Korean army reached the Yalu River on the Korean side, but without intending to cross the river into China.

China Sends So-Called Chinese People's Volunteers Into Korea

As the South Korean army did not enter the territory of China, according to reason and international law, the Communist Party of China should not send its army into Korea. However, the so-called Chinese People's Volunteers crossed the river into Korea. Could this also be called an invasion? At first Marshal Lin Biao (There were 10 marshals in China) was appointed the commander of the Chinese People's Volunteers, but he refused to take the assignment. Marshal Peng Dehuai took the position of the commander. The eldest son of Mao Zedong joined the Volunteers, though not as a fighter. No one knew why Mao let his son join. When the son died accidentally, it was said that Mao blamed Marshal Peng for it, for not providing adequate protection for his son.

The Chinese forces seriously savaged a battalion of the South Korean army near Onjong. In this battle the first Chinese prisoners of war were captured. Then Chinese soldiers attacked the 6th Infantry Division of the South Korean army. Although the US Air Force bombarded the bridges on the Yalu River, the Chinese soldiers used pontoon bridges and even crossed the river by walking on the thick ice. Toward the end of November, the Chinese army doubled its numbers and fiercely attacked the United Nations army and stopped their further advance. Then the Eighth Army in northwest Korea and the X Corps in northeast Korea withdrew southward and at last were back to the 38th parallel. The X Corps withdrew by sea. The thick snow provided a good cover for the targets in North Korea.

Some US troops were surrounded by the outnumbered Chinese army in the Changjin Reservoir area. The US troops fought their way to Hagaru-ri, and at the same time a relief column from Hungnam marched toward the troops, reaching Koto-ri almost seven miles away. The Chinese army, in great numbers, prevented the two groups from uniting and surrounded both respectively. The US troops were only receiving air supplies. The US units tried to break out from Hagaru-ri and Koto-ri, and finally they linked up. Then eight C-119s dropped bridge spans to the encircled US units so that they could cross a 1500-foot-deep gorge to break the encirclement of the Chinese army.

Toward the end of December 1950, the Chinese forces crossed the 38th parallel and assaulted the United Nations troops. The Eighth Army built their defensive line 70 miles from the 38th parallel. Just at the beginning of the new year, 1951, almost half a million Chinese and North Korean army took a new ground offensive, and so the Fifth Air force raided their troop column. As great numbers of Chinese troops advanced, the Eighth Army began to evacuate from Seoul, the capital of South Korea. The South Korean government moved to Pusan. Seoul changed hands again as the Chinese troops rushed in. In the mid-January, the Chinese army took Wonju, reaching their farthest extent of advance into South Korea.

To disrupt a new offensive of the Chinese army, the US X Corps marched forth, aided by air support, to near Hoengsong. On the east coast the troops of South Korea crossed the 38th parallel and entered Yangyang. In mid-February, three Chinese divisions surrounded the United Nations troops, including members of the US 23rd Regimental Combat Team and the French Battalion at a road junction of Chipyong-ni in the central Korea. But a few days later, the Eighth Army wiped out a large number of Chinese troops and moved the United Nations line northward to the Han River. Therefore, the Chinese army had no presence on the south side of the river. The Communist Party of China always used the same trick to wipe out their opponents, but this time their own army was wiped out.

In mid-March, the Chinese forces abandoned Seoul without resistance when the US troops seized the high ground on both sides of the city north of the Han River. Then US air transports, flying from Taegu to Munsan-ni, a region behind Chinese lines some 20 miles northwest of Seoul, dropped the 187th Airborne Regimental Combat Team and two Ranger companies—more than 3,400 men. The Fifth Air Force fighters and light bombers conquered the opposition of the Chinese army, and so the United Nations forces marched rapidly to the Imjin River, capturing 127 Chinese prisoners of war. The Eighth Army moved northward across the 38th parallel.

With the coming of spring, the Chinese launched an all-out offensive with over 330,000 troops, using their "human wave" tactics. By the end of this month, they advanced to the vicinity of Seoul again. But under the United Nations assaults on the ground and in the air, both men and supplies on the Chinese side reached their limits. So the Eighth Army successfully stopped their further progress.

In spite of the resistance of the Chinese and North Korean army, the United Nations forces broke into the Pyonggang-Chorwon-Kumhwa "Iron Triangle" fortified sanctuaries just north of the 38th parallel. Therefore, on the 23rd of June, Jacob Malik, the Soviet Ambassador to the United Nations, called for negotiations between the representatives of the United Nations forces and those of the Chinese and North Korean forces for an armistice in Korea based on the separation of the armies along the 38th parallel.

On the 10th of July, Vice Admiral Turner Joy, leading the United Nations delegation met the Chinese and North Korean delegation at Kaesong, some 30 miles northwest of Seoul on the south side of the 38th parallel, for the first conference of the armistice negotiations. Therefore, less actions on the ground and in the air was maintained. But on the 4th of August, the Chinese ground forces violated the Kaesong neutral zone, resulting in suspension of the truce talks. Then on the 10th of August the armistice negotiations resumed at Kaesong with the North Korea promise to respect the neutral zone. However, on the 22nd of August, the Chinese and North Korean delegation trumped up evidence that a United Nations aircraft bombed Kaesong (not considering the safety of their own delegation?), which resulted in the suspension of the armistice negotiations once again.

Then actions on the ground and in the air resumed. United Nations ground forces withstood the battalion-sized attacks of the Chinese army in the "Punchbowl", the circular valley in the eastern Korea, west of the Soyang River and rimmed by sharply rising hills. On the 25th of October, at the request of the Chinese and North Korean delegation, the peace negotiations resumed at Kaesong after a two-month suspension. By that time the United Nations ground forces in the western and central sections had gained up to six miles in some places along the frontline.

On the 12th of November, the peace negotiations moved to Panmunjom, a village less than 5 miles east of Kaesong, in a newly established demilitarized zone on the 38th parallel. The United Nations forces ceased offensive ground operations. Toward the end of 1951, the negotiators at Panmunjom argued over the arrangements for an armistice and provisions about the prisoners of war. Ground actions of both sides reduced to minimum. However, at Panmunjom, the negotiations made no progress. To prevent the further attack of the Chinese and North Korean army in the frontline, the main strategy of the United Nations was to hinder the transportation of equipment and supplies to their front positions. So the targets of the air raid concentrated on bridges on rivers, railroads, moving trains and trucks.

In April of 1952, there were two major ground engagements. The Chinese and North Korean forces attacked at night the positions held by the First Marine Division south of Panmunjom and later assaulted the First Commonwealth Division north of Korangpo-ri. The friendly units withstood these attacks. No other ground actions happened this month.

In June, US 45th Infantry Division in the central sector near Chorwon launched two attacks successfully to gain a high ground and repulsed the counterattack of the Chinese troops. But in July, in the eastern sector of Korea, near the coast and near Hill 266 in the US Second Infantry Division area, a battalion of the Chinese army attempted to seize the high ground. It changed hands several times, but remained under the friendly control at the end of the month.

In mid-August, some reinforced-battalions of the Chinese army attacked the United Nations positions in several sectors. Hills in the First Marine Division sector and in the South Korean Second Corps sector changed hands several times, but United Nations forces retained control of those sectors.

On the 29th of August, at the request of the US Department of State, US Far East Air Force launched the largest air attack against Pyongyang to serve as a dramatic military action during the visit of China's premier, Zhou Enlai, to the Soviet Union. The State Department hoped that the attack might lead the Soviets to urge the Chinese to accept an armistice in the peace negotiations at Panmunjom.

In September, the heaviest ground activity centered in the sector of the Second Corps of South Korean army with intense seesaw fighting, but effected little change in the front lines.

Between the 6th day and the 15th of October, the Chinese ground forces assaulted chiefly in the western IX Corps area northwest of Chorwon in a vain attempt to improve their position before the onslaught of winter. In mid-October, the Eighth Army launched an offensive to seize critical high ground in eastern IX Corps area northeast of Kumhwa. But it became a seesaw contest to retain domination terrain.

On the 8th of October, truce talks at Panmunjom recessed over the issue of forced repatriation of the prisoners of war. The United Nations delegates proposed allowing the prisoners of war from opposite sides to choose repatriation or not, but the Chinese and North Korean delegates insisted that all prisoners of war be repatriated.

On the 16th of October, 1952, North Korea sent a strongly worded protest to the Far East Command concerning the recess in armistice negotiations, but they continued to insist on total repatriation of both Chinese and North Korean prisoners of war. At the end of this month they presented a new prisoners-of-war camp list. In Geneva, the League of Red Cross Societies recommended that the combatants exchange sick and wounded prisoners of war before the cease-fire.

On the 22nd of January in 1953, Beijing radio announced the capture of Colonel Arnold, pilot of a B-29 who was shot down on January 13. But the Chinese government refused to release him even during the repatriation of war prisoners. He was released in 1956.

On the 22nd of February, in a letter to Kim Il Sung, Premier of North Korea government and Marshal Peng Dehuai, Chinese commander in North Korea, the United Nations command stated its readiness to immediately repatriate those seriously ill and wounded prisoners of war who were fit to travel, and asked whether the North Korea and Chinese leaders were prepared to do the same.

During the first half of March, the Chinese army attacked in company-sized waves in several areas, particularly along the central front in the Kumhwa and Kumsong regions. Later, sometimes, they attacked by the regiment in the central and western sectors. Then US Intelligence found the military strength of the Chinese army growing, with from one to three Chinese divisions en route to or entering the Korean peninsula. The buildup indicated a possible offensive to seize as much territory as possible before the armistice.

On March 21, North Korean truce negotiators expressed their willingness to observe the provisions of the Geneva Convention and exchange sick and wounded prisoners. At the same time they hinted that the exchange might lead to a resolution of other issues that had hindered the armistice so far.

On March 30, Zhou Enlai, the foreign minister of China, suggested that prisoners of war not desiring repatriation might be

placed in the temporary custody of a neutral nation until negotiations determined their final status. Before his proposal, they
had insisted on repatriating all the prisoners of war. Their new
flexibility on this issue provided an opportunity to resume truce
negotiations.

On the 26th of April, after suspension for six months, armistice negotiations between the Chinese and North Korean
delegation and the United Nations delegation reconvened in
Panmunjom. Representatives of both sides negotiated details of
the repatriation of prisoners of war. Then there followed the exchange of the seriously wounded and sick prisoners—6670 Chinese and North Koreans for 471 South Koreans, 149 Americans,
and 64 other United Nations personnel, the count at that time.

US aircraft spread leaflets in North Korea, announcing that
anyone who delivered a MiG or other jet aircraft to the United Nations forces in South Korea would receive political asylum, resettlement in a noncommunist country, anonymity, and
$50,000. An additional $50,000 bounty would go to the first
person to take advantage of this offer. In September 1953, after
the cease-fire, a North Korean MiG-15 pilot flew his aircraft
safely to Kimpo air base in South Korea.

In the last week of May, the Chinese and North Korean troops
made a major ground offensive against the United Nations positions on ridges dominating the US I Corps sector, about 10 miles
northeast of Panmunjom. Meanwhile, the armistice negotiations faltered over disagreements regarding the repatriation of
the prisoners of war. The Chinese and North Korean delegates
wanted North Korean prisoners unwilling to return to their
homelands to be detained indefinitely, in effect punishing them
for their decision. The United Nations delegates wanted to release all prisoners to civilian status on the day the armistice
became effective. To let the Chinese and North Koreans know
that the continuance of the war would incur additional political
and economic costs, the US Air Force attacked targets in North
Korea that had been untouched previously. They bombed irrigation dams, whose destruction would, besides interrupting food
production, disrupt further preparations for a ground offensive
on the part of the Chinese and North Korean army by flooding
the rails and road networks.

By mid-June, both sides had agreed to establish a Neutral Nations Repatriation committee. The final session of armistice negotiations at Panmunjom convened. After meeting for one day, the top negotiators agreed to adjourn while technical experts worked out the cease-fire details.

At 10:00AM on July 27, 1953, the armistice agreement was signed to produce the cease-fire in the Korean War between the United Nations forces, South Korea, and the Chinese People's Volunteers, North Korea. In accordance with the armistice agreement, in August, the prisoners of war were exchanged in Operation Big Switch—77,000 Chinese and North Korean army prisoners of war, for 12,700 prisoners from the United Nations and South Korean army, including 3,597 Americans, the final count.

(The above data was taken from the US government booklet entitled "The USAF in Korea".)

CHAPTER 10. THE 3 ANTI-'S AND 5 ANTI-'S MOVEMENTS

The 3 Anti-'s Movement

In November 1951, two party secretaries in Tianjin were caught embezzling funds. Therefore, on December 1, 1951, the Central Committee of the Communist Party launched the cost-saving movement which was literally called "Three Anti-'s": anti-embezzlement, anti-waste, and anti-bureaucratism. This movement was targeted at cadres of the government and government-run enterprises; the ones who had power. Mao wanted to clip their wings. At that time, there were 3,830,000 government cadres. They would be examined through this movement.

The cadres could be divided into three categories. The first were those who had gone through the Sino–Japanese war and the second civil war, who should be dependable. The second category included those newly employed after the establishment of the new republic. The third group were those having worked in the former government, who were undependable, of course. Those who were guilty of the crime of embezzlement were called "tigers." Through this movement, the Communist Party wanted to "catch big tigers" so that there would not be any embezzlement in the government any more. Anyone who embezzled 10,000 yuan was defined as a big tiger and would be executed. In China, political movements were often carried out with violence. So many targeted persons committed suicide, even though they were cadres.

The 5 Anti-'s Movement

Right in the wake of the three Anti-'s movement, another program was launched, which was literally called "Five Anti-'s": anti-bribery, anti-tax-evasion, anti-jerry-rigging, anti-stealing-government-property, and anti-theft-of-government-economic-information. The target of this movement was all the national capitalists; the ones who had money. In feudal societies like Imperial China, the emperor considered that everything on the land he ruled over was his own, and everyone on this land essentially worked for him. Verbally, Mao declared himself as a Marxist-Leninist, but his actions often made him look like the "communist emperor of the Red Dynasty." His actions showed people what he thought; he didn't put it in plain words. And given the low level of development and widespread poverty in China, the Communists under Mao sought to cover the basic necessities of life for everyone; and that didn't leave much extra. All excesses would be confiscated.

On the 26th of January, 1952, the Central Committee of the Communist Party issued instructions for the Five-Anti-'s movement. In early February, it started in all the big cities, aiming at businessmen. The Party defined them as capitalists. The Party divided Chinese capitalists into two types: bureaucratic capitalists like Chiang Kai-shek, Soong Tse-ven, K'ung Hsiang-hsi, and the Chen brothers, who were very wealthy and were called the four big capitalist families. All the property they left on the mainland was confiscated. All others were defined as national capitalists, and their properties remained with them for the time being. Now they were the target of the five anti-'s movement.

The local governments organized so-called work teams consisting of cadres, workers and shop assistants. Violence was part of every movement. Some capitalists were beaten or slapped in their faces. Capitalists were forced to confess what they had failed to do so far in these five categories. This was called 'face to face fight.' Quite a few capitalists committed suicide. Then the government changed from face-to-face fight to a back-to-back tactic. Workers or shop assistants just revealed the crimes of their bosses, behind their backs, so that no retaliation could be inflicted.

Statistics showed that during these two movements, in the whole country, 184,270 persons were arrested, 119,355 party members expelled, and 133,760 people were killed or disabled, including those committing suicide or beaten to death, or tortured to death in jails and labor reform camps. Those who committed suicide were mostly capitalists. The means of suicide were various. In some secluded corners of public parks, people were found hanging from big trees. Then, patrols increased to prevent hangings in such places. The most popular method of suicide was to jump from high buildings. It was the easiest way, and hard to prevent. But it was dangerous for pedestrians. A person who jumped from a height could possibly fall on the head of a pedestrian and the pedestrian could be killed, while the one jumping survived. Someone actually did some research to see why people in Shanghai did not jump into the Wangpu River. The answer was that if anyone jumped into the river, he could possibly be saved; besides, if he was not saved his body would be washed out to sea. When his body was not found, the government would suspect him of escaping outside the country and his family would get into trouble. So he had to leave his body to be found. Generally a suicide would leave a note, in which he first criticized himself for whatever crime he had been accused of, then he praised the government so that his family would be treated a little better than otherwise. Poor Chinese people! Even suicide was fraught with difficulties.

Both of the "Anti" movements ended in October 1952.

At the end of the 5 Anti-'s movement, the government determined that every national capitalist had at least committed the crime of tax-evasion and would have to pay a big fine to the government. So all the capitalists had to sell personal belongings like cars, jewelry, or even houses, if they did not have enough cash in the bank. That was the first financial blow to the national capitalists. Another financial blow would soon follow.

Mao's Own Lifestyle

Mao wanted government officials to save money and he took money out of the pockets of the well-to-do. Thus his own spending raised a lot of questions in some people's minds. He could spend as much as he saw fit. He ordered many villas to be built for his own use only. They were needed, apparently, to provide the best protection and comfort for him. He had over 50 villas in the country, 5 in Beijing alone. The villas were all similarly built: looking like a big cement warehouse from outside, but one that could protect him even from an atom bomb. Every villa, or bunker, was only one storey tall, but they were located in beautiful settings, some with lakes. The whole surroundings were enclosed. In the vicinity of every villa, a transportation network was built, such as a military airport, a train line, and a tunnel for cars. Wherever Mao went, the three means of transportation followed him. When he rode in his personal airplane, the airspace would be cleared while his plane flew past. When he rode in his personal train, other trains had to stop while his train went past.

CHAPTER 11. THE SO-CALLED GAO GANG & RAO SHUSHI ANTI-PARTY EVENT

Mao was familiar with Chinese political history. When certain new dynasties began, the first emperors of those dynasties would find fault with some of their faithful supporters who were deemed by those emperors to be potential threats to their future as rulers. Therefore, those supporters were killed or imprisoned for whatever possible crimes could be attributed to them. So was the case with Gao Gang and Rao Shushi.

Gao (1905–1954) came from a poor peasant family in Shaanxi province. In January, 1927, he entered the Yat-sen Military Academy in XiAn and joined the Communist Party in February. In 1933, he was the political commissar of the 42nd division of the Red 26th army. In the Communist Army system, a political commissar was the representative of the Communist Party in the army, a little higher in rank than the division commander. Then he was appointed director of the political department in the Red 15th corps. But in 1935, he was imprisoned as a reactionary and was about to be executed. Just at that time, Mao and Zhou Enlai reached the northern Shaanxi province, with the central Red Army. Mao ordered Gao to be released and Gao was so grateful to Mao he became Mao's faithful supporter ever after. So in the 7th conference of the Communist Party, he became a member of the Central Political Bureau (equivalent to the executive depart-

ment of the Central Committee) and the secretary of the northwest bureau. (All over the country, the Communist Party set up
six bureaus. Every bureau rules over several provinces.)

After Japan surrendered, the Communist Party intended to
occupy the northeastern provinces and set up a northeast bureau. Gao was appointed the secretary to take charge of everything in that region. In 1946, Lin Biao was sent up to the northeastern provinces as the commander of the 4th field army and he
worked with Gao in a cooperative relationship. Often they both
had the same view. After the new republic was established, Gao
was the vice chairman of the central people's government, the
vice chairman of the people's revolutionary military committee,
and also the chairman of the people's government in the northeastern area. After the Korean War broke out, though Gao disagreed on sending the Chinese army into Korea, he still gave full
support in supplying whatever the army needed there. So Marshal Peng Dehuai praised him for that. Gao was also the chairman of the national planning committee—clearly, a very capable
man.

Rao Shushi (1903–1975) was born in Jiangxi province. He
joined the Communist Party in 1925. Then he was made the secretary of the party caucus of the Federation of Labor Unions of
Shanghai and the secretary of the party caucus of the Chinese
National General Labor Union. During the Anti-Japanese war,
he was the political commissar of the new 4th army. During the
second civil war, he was the political commissar of the 3rd field
army and the secretary of the east China bureau of the Communist Party. When the new republic was founded, he was the
chairman of the east China military and political committee, the
first secretary of the east China bureau, and then the minister of
the organization department of the Central Committee of the
Communist Party. Also an intelligent, qualified leader.

Gao's and Rao's paths in life had never crossed each other;
they were in different regions entirely. But they were both accused of the crime of being anti-Party together. Anyway, why
were they not accused of being anti-Party separately? It was understood that no man could act against the Communist Party of
China, only a clique could try that. And you need at least two
powerful persons to form a clique (the same held true during

the Cultural Revolution, when Liu Shaoqi and Deng Xiaoping were put together as the powerful men accused of following the capitalist road).

In accordance with the official statement of the Communist Party, the main accusations against Gao were: criticizing mistakes and errors in the national economic field, namely decisions concerning Liu Shaoqi and Zhou Enlai, members of the Secretariat of the CPC (Communist Party of China) Central Committee in charge of that field. From the same source, Gao was understood to have further slandered them by saying that Liu and Zhou Enlai had cliques in the Central Committee. Gao and Rao were alleged to have spread a rumor that An Ziwen, the vice minister of the organization department of the CPC Central Committee, had put up a list of the members of the CPC political bureau, at the instruction of Liu. (That meant that Liu privately let An make such a list behind the back of Mao.) Then Gao left Beijing on a vacation to see Deng Xiaoping, Chen Yun and Lin Biao separately and tried to persuade them to support him. What would his purpose have been? The official statement alleged that Gao wanted to replace Liu in his higher political position. But why would Rao work with Gao? What could Rao get from it? The official statement said that Rao wanted to acquire the power to appoint and promote the cadres. But at that time Rao was already the minister of the organization department of the CPC Central Committee and already had that power.

In 1951, Gao thought of publishing an article he had written as an editorial in the *Northeast Daily*, but rather than take it upon himself to do so of his own accord, he handed in the article for Mao to read and give his approval first. Think of that. Historians surmise that Mao did want to get rid of Liu, which he did in the Cultural Revolution, but at that time, the conditions were not yet ripe. Conceivably Gao got the wind of it and acted earlier than Mao planned. Mao had to get rid of him lest his cat got out of the bag.

Another surmise, which came from Khrushchev's memoirs, was that Gao had sent information to the Soviet Union about things that were going on in the Communist Party of China and what the leaders said. The Soviet Union had provided China with old, rebuilt tanks, and some such things, and the Chinese leaders were dissatisfied. Those leaders included Liu and Zhou. Gao did not mention Mao. To secure Mao's trust and friendship, Stalin gave Mao the information he had received from Gao. Therefore, Mao wanted to get rid of Gao (but why was Rao included?) and made arrangements with Liu and Zhou. Mao gave Gao the false impression that he wanted to rid Liu, or even hinted that Gao should do something about it. Gao, thinking that he had Mao's support, fell into the snare Mao set up for him. Gao was then taken into custody. He attempted a suicide in April 1954, but in vain. He made another suicide attempt in August and died this time. Rao was apprehended on April 1, 1955, and sentenced to 14 years. After 10 years he was out of the jail, but was put back in again during the Cultural Revolution and died on March 2, 1975.

It was said that Rao was arrested due to his involvement in another case. During the movement to arrest and kill the reactionaries, Yang Fan, the chief of the police station of Shanghai, thought of a method to use reactionaries to reveal hidden reactionaries. In the process, he did not punish those he utilized and so he was accused of protecting reactionaries—more than 3,300 in number. This involved Rao. Moreover, Pan Hannian, a vice mayor of Shanghai in charge of police affairs, feared that since he had worked with Rao and Yang Fan, he would have to confess his side of the story to the Party so that he might ride out the crisis. He confessed that in the summer of 1943, he went to Shanghai from where the new 4th army was encamped to meet Li Shiqun, a traitor to Japan, and he was kidnapped and taken to Nanking to see Wang Jingwei. Although he did not betray the Communist Party, when he was back at the camp he did not report to the Party what had happened. Now he confessed it and was arrested. Then Rao Shushi, Pan Hannian and Yang Fan were defined as an anti-Party clique. This clique was separate from the Gao Gang clique.

After the Cultural Revolution, some cases were re-opened and examined. Pan was sent by the Party to contact the traitor Li to get information. So his case was redressed, and also the case of Yang Fan. Now what about Gao's and Rao's "anti-Party" activities? When Gao had sought Deng Xiaoping's support against Liu Shaoqi, Deng reported to Mao, and Gao was imprisoned. If Gao's case was wrong, it shows that Mao's decision to confine

Gao was wrong and Deng's report to Mao was also wrong. After the Cultural Revolution, Deng Xiaoping was in power and he would never admit that he had done anything wrong, to save face. So the case was not redressed.

CHAPTER 12. CHINA'S FIRST FIVE-YEAR PLAN (1953–57)

Agricultural Collectivization and Peasant Cooperatives

As the basis for their ambitious economic planning, the CPC held China's first modern census in 1952. The mainland population was estimated at over half a billion—that's a lot of mouths to feed. The first step toward improving efficiency and productivity involved land reforms.

During the land reform movement, first the arable land was taken from wealthy individuals and distributed to individual peasants and their families. But then the Communist Party called upon peasants to join productive cooperatives, on a "voluntary" basis but with invisible political pressure behind it. Once they joined the cooperative, peasants lost control of their land, which automatically belonged to the cooperative. The cooperative would decide what crops to grow and when harvests were sold, peasants got a certain percentage of income according to the quantity of the land a peasant put in. When a peasant had his land under his own control, he could decide what to grow and what part of the harvest he would keep for his own use, and the rest he would sell in the market.

By the end of 1952, the first 3,600 cooperatives were operating on a trial basis. On the 16th of December, 1953, the Central Committee of the CPC passed a bill to speed up the development of agricultural productive cooperatives. From 1954 to the first half of 1955, cooperatives sprang up all over the country. In spring of 1954, there were already 95,000 cooperatives, which meant that 1,700,000 families had joined them. In autumn of the same year, the cooperatives had increased to more than 225,000. On May 17, 1955, at Mao's proposal, the Central Committee of the CPC decided to expand the cooperatives to one million in 1956. By July of 1955, the cooperatives reached the number of 650,000 and by the end of 1956, 96.3% of peasant families had joined the cooperatives.

That was the essential change of the agricultural productive style from individual to collective. This process roughly coincided with the consolidation of America's private farms into a large-scale industrial agro business which was carried out by capitalist means involving loans and debt, price manipulation and other methods. Different means to pursue the same end, although not with the same results.

Private Businesses Become State Property

The economical ideal of the Communist Party was that there should be no private businesses in a so-called socialist country. Private businesses were the typical symbol of the capitalist system. So at the end of 1955, Chen Yun, in charge of the national economy, declared a reform of private businesses over the next two years. Then Peng Zhen, the mayor of Beijing, proposed to finish the reform in 1956 in Beijing. In January of 1956, in just a few days, Beijing completed the reform. Mao pushed it by visiting a textile factory owned by Rong Yiren, the biggest national capitalist in China at the time, on the 10th of January. Rong offered to turn over his factories to government ownership on the 20th. Others followed suit, in all cities where there were private businesses.

The carefully-formulated process was that the private business owner must send in an application begging the communist government to take over his business. Accordingly the government would approve his application. This was like a traveler offering his belongings to an outlaw and begging him to take them. The outlaw was only willing to accept the offer for mercy's sake, as if the belongings were so heavy they would break the traveler's back if he carried them any longer. The outlaw was only relieving him of a burden.

Anyway, in Beijing, on the 15th of January, 1956, there was a celebration on TianAnMen Square where 200,000 people gathered to celebrate the completion of the takeover of private businesses by the government. The takeover was called a "purchasing policy," which meant that the government bought these private businesses from the private owners and paid them a certain amount of money called "fixed interests," which would be paid off at the annual rate of 5% of the value of these private businesses. The government decided what was the value of a factory or a store, and the owner had no right to bargain. As a rule, the government should have paid the owner for 20 years at the rate of 5%, but no, the government promised to pay only for 7 years. And at the end of the 7 years it would make a further decision to see whether it would continue to pay or not. Anyway, this sounded better than outright expropriation.

This was the second financial blow to the national capitalists, leaving them only their personal belongings like jewelry and antiques, if they had any left after paying fines. But the final financial blow was coming soon.

The payment of fixed interests might last for 3 years more, which meant the government only paid for 10 years out of the 20 years, only half of the value.

After these takeovers, the former owner would be given a position in the business (as a salesman or other worker). If he was accorded a position like manager, he was only holding the position in name, and had no say whatsoever in the decisions. The party secretary was the one to decide everything, even if he understood nothing about the business. Older owners just retired and lived on the fixed interests while the younger ones accepted their salary as well as the fixed interests.

CHAPTER 13. SO-CALLED THREE RED BANNERS

The purpose of the slogan "Three Red Banners" was to help make China a strong and prosperous country in the shortest possible period by building "socialism with Chinese characteristics," that is, by avoiding certain limitations built into other nations' experiments with communist/socialist models.

Every dynasty in Chinese history favored a particular color. For the Qing Dynasty, yellow (or gold) symbolized the imperial authority. The Communist Party has always favored red. Initially that red was meant to symbolize the blood of martyred revolutionaries, but over time this image has been broadened in some people's view to include the blood of those bystanders who became victims to the various campaigns through which regime change was accomplished.

Anyway, the "three red banners" meant the General Line (for socialist construction), the Great Leap Forward, and the People's Commune.

The General Line

The General Line was "to keep up full energy, to fight your way upstream, and to build socialism quickly and thriftily, abundantly and well." On October 11, 1955, Mao said at a meeting that the cooperatives must be developed abundantly, quick-ly and well. Then Li Fuchun (1900–1975), vice director of the plan committee and vice Premier of the state council, suggested adding "thriftily", which was accepted. So on January 1, 1956, the *People's Daily* ran an editorial urging the people to keep this theme in mind while carrying out the first five-year plan. In 1958, the *People's Daily* New Year's day editorial exhorted the populace to continue working with their full energy, to strive to get up-stream. So the General Line was formed. In theory, it was a good mission statement (to use today's terminology). But, in carrying it out, the Communist Party went astray and moved contrary to the reality of how processes unfold, and this was true as well in the so-called Great Leap forward and the People's Commune movements.

The Great Leap Forward

On the 29th of June, 1957, an article was published with the signature of one Yu Jianhui, in which the slogan of "the Great Leap Forward" was first heard. In September, during the Third Plenary Session of the Eighth Central Committee of the CPC, the decision was made to carry out the Great Leap Forward movement in agriculture. On the 13th of November, the editorial of the *People's Daily* said, "Some people are infected with Right-deviationist conservatism and have crawled like snails. Since the agricultural collectivization has taken place, we have all the con-ditions and the necessities to make the Great Leap Forward on the productivity front." On the 2nd of February, 1958, the slogan of an overall Great Leap Forward was emphasized more broadly.

In spring of 1958, major moves were made for the building of agricultural irrigation systems and for the collection of natural fertilizer on a large scale in the countryside. For irrigation con-struction, the labor force used reached 20 or 30 million workers in October, and 80 million in December. In January of 1958, it reached 100 million. Some provinces that produced mostly in-dustrial goods guaranteed they would produce enough grain, meat and vegetables for the people in those provinces in that year. Formerly, these had been brought in from other provinces. This was considered the prelude to the Great Leap Forward. In the countryside the Great Leap Forward was linked with the people's commune movement.

The People's Commune

Mao wanted to enlarge the cooperative commune into the so-called People's Commune. On July 1, 1958, the first People's Commune was established, merging 27 cooperatives, with 9,360 families involved, in Henan Province. Its official name was Chayashan Satellite People's Commune. The commune was really a basic local government. It controlled almost everything in the district of the commune, from agricultural production to people's daily life. It had public canteens—no more eating at home, as a family—kindergartens, clinics, shops, and its own armed forces (called militia) instead of police.

As peasants no longer had their own land and worked for the commune, for very low pay, their enthusiasm for work was essentially quenched. The Party admitted later that it was a mistake, a wrong policy. In order to increase productivity, in 1958, the professor and rocket scientist Qian Xuesen created a theory of "High Productivity," on the basis of calculation only, without any practical investigation. He was not an agronomist nor a plant physiologist, but he wanted to fulfill Mao's desire and invented a suitable theory. It was called "high productivity satellite." When Mao learned of the theory, he gave instructions that all the communes should implement the theory. But the land could not yield as much as had been calculated theoretically. Therefore, false statistics were reported to the Party. From June to November, high production was reported thirty-nine times. The highest yield of wheat was 7,320 catties (about 24 tons) per acre, that of corn 117 tons per acre, and similarly exaggerated statistics for rice, sweet potato, etc. Possibly, Mao believed some of this; but people generally got the impression that everything said in the news was misleading.

As it was reported that the peasants had produced so much grain, Mao and other Party leaders worried about what to do with it all. Mao said the peasants could eat all they wanted, for free, and if the people could not consume so much, they would be able to give the surplus to foreign people.

They also wanted people in cities to organize people's communes. In every block, the resident committee had to have a canteen so that the residents could go there for meals, like in the countryside. But most of the city residents did not eat in the canteens. They still cooked at home. So the city people's commune was a quick failure. Then Mao criticized himself, saying that he had listened to Qian as if he had no brains of his own. Even Tian Jiaying, his secretary, asked him how, coming from a peasant family himself, he could have believed that it was possible to produce such vast quantities of food per acre. It seems that Mao had no grasp of science or mathematics. Qian Xuesen actually did have plenty of brains. He was a US-educated rocket scientist who helped establish the Jet Propulsion Laboratory before being deported in 1955 as a Communist. He went on to build China's own space program, from intercontinental ballistic missiles and satellites to putting a man in space in 2003.

Mao was in a hurry to bring to life "communist society" before his death. Mao forced the nation to implement his ideas even when they were ill-founded, and as a result, the whole nation sank into economical disaster. Things became scarce, especially food. People in cities were quickly put on rations and had to use their limited coupons to buy all the necessities such as rice, flour, meat, eggs, cloth, cooking oil, sugar, cigarettes, matches, yarn or thread, products based on bean curd, and even bathroom tissue. There were also ration coupons to buy cakes, biscuits, or anything made from rice or flour. If anyone went to a restaurant and ate rice or noodles, he had to give rice coupons besides paying money. The cashiers' work was made a little more complicated, as they had to calculate the money as well as the coupons.

Ration coupons were distributed according to the number of persons in a family, and were given to the family every three months. At the beginning of every quarter, housewives waited in expectation of the distribution of coupons to buy everything they needed. Every family had two small booklets, one to buy rice or flour in grain stores (with a certain limit) if they wanted to cook rice or use flour in any kind of recipe at home, and the other used to buy coal to fuel the cooking ovens. The "Three Red Banners" ended in failure.

CHAPTER 14. SOVIET EXPERTS GIVE TECHNICAL ASSISTANCE

Soviet Counselors and Experts Help China

The Communist Party was aware that China was very backward and had few technicians and scientists who could take the lead in economical development when they took over the country. Therefore, they asked the Soviet Union for help. In 1949, the Soviet Union sent Anastas Ivanovich Mikoyan, member of the Bolshevik politburo, on a secret visit to Xibopo where the headquarters of the Liberation Army had moved in May 1948. Stalin wanted to know, first, what attitude the Communist Party of China would hold towards the Soviet Union. At the same time he talked about possible technical aid to China after the Communist Party of China expressed their willingness to accept Soviet leadership. At a meeting on February 1, Zhou Enlai requested the Soviet Union to send experts and equipment for weapons manufacture, and advisors to train troops and help to set up military academies." Mikoyan could not give any answer but reported to Stalin, and asked the Communist Party of China send a delegation to the Soviet Union for further discussion. In June 1949, Liu Shaoqi headed a secret delegation to Moscow. In August, 220 Soviet financial advisors and engineers came to

China with him. At that time in northern China, 1,300,000 out of 1,500,000 cadres were illiterate. So it was very important to have Soviet experts come in.

Besides sending Chinese cadres to the Soviet Union for training and practical experience, the Communist Party of China invited many Soviet experts to manage almost every department of the central government, from security, military, and intelligence, to gymnastics and hygiene. There were over 400 Soviet advisors in the central government, one third of all the advisors and experts in China. According to Soviet statistics, during 1951–1953, there were 1210 Soviet experts working in China. A report from the Communist Party of China of China revealed that Soviet experts helped to build 51 factories by April of 1953, and from 1953 to 1959, 91 factories were built. The Soviet experts assumed the duties of selecting sites for the factories, the design, and the supply of equipment. They instructed Chinese workers how to install the equipment and how to operate it and manufacture new products. In one report, Li Fuchun said, "Without the assistance of the Soviet Union, we would not have achieved such speed and scale in our construction in the first five-year plan. We would certainly have faced unimaginable difficulties."

The Soviets With Their Advisors and Experts

But in the Korean War, the Soviet Union sold China out-of-date and unusable weaponry. During 1950–1951, one fourth of the airplanes that were delivered to China were not flight-ready but needed repairs. So towards the end of the first five-year plan, the Communist Party adjusted its policy on the use of Soviet advisors and experts. At a meeting in Chengdu city, in March of 1958, Mao criticized the blind worship of Soviet experts and demanded that his people push back against dogmatism and slave-like thinking. This change in Mao's attitude towards the Soviet Union was after the death of Stalin in 1953. Stalin was openly acknowledged as the leader of the Communist International movements. Although Mao thought highly of himself, he did not dare to challenge Stalin for the international leadership position. Since Stalin was gone, Mao had no great esteem for the new Soviet leader. He thought that he himself should replace Stalin as the leader of world Communism.

In August 1958, Khrushchev, the new head of the Soviet Union, visited Beijing and held talks with Mao. One might conclude from this visit that Mao thought he held a more important position in the communist world so that Khrushchev should come to Beijing to see him. If Stalin were still alive, it certainly would have been Mao who went to Moscow for any talks. Stalin would never have come to Beijing. Anyway, Mao and Khrushchev had different opinions about the need for Soviet advisors and experts. Mao could not tolerate having Soviet advisors intervene so deeply in China's affairs and wanted to reduce their number, but he still needed the technical experts. So the number of the advisors and experts decreased year by year: 952 in 1957, 915 in 1958, 699 in 1959, and 410 in 1960.

The tension between the Communist Party of China and the Soviet Communist Party became open during the Bucharest conference in June 1960. Khrushchev and Peng Zhen, head of the Chinese delegation, had a quarrel. The Soviet Union accused China of violating their agreement to present a unified front, not displaying the difference in views between the two parties and the Chinese opposition to the common route supported by the communist world. Only Albania stood with China. After the conference, the Soviet Union withdrew all its advisors and experts from China, leaving many tasks unfinished. The notion of an unbreakable friendship between the Soviet Union and China was over.

CHAPTER 15. THE ANTI-RIGHTIST MOVEMENT

Let a Hundred Flowers Bloom

In April 1956, Mao gave a speech introducing the "Double-Hundred Policy," the meaning of which was "To let a hundred flowers bloom, let a hundred (different) opinions be expressed." Then the Minister for Propaganda, Lu Dingyi, made a speech explaining to all the intellectuals that they should go ahead and think independently. They would have freedom to debate and criticize, creative freedom, freedom of expression, and the right to their own opinions. It was so sweet to hear that many believed it; but only fools gave out their opinions boldly.

On May 1, 1957, the *People's Daily* published "Instructions about the Rectification Movement," which had been passed at the Central Committee of the Communist Party on April 27. The Party had decided to start a rectification movement within the Party to foster anti-bureaucratism, anti-sectarianism, and anti-subjectivism. The Party called upon people outside the Party, upon people the country over, to express their opinions, to criticize the Party and government, and to help the Party to rectify any shortcomings. The request sounded earnest. This was the sole movement that was aimed at improving the Party itself.

Many people in the country, especially the intellectuals, educated people (which included many of the capitalists, or propertied class), all those and other fools, did criticize the Party for their so many obvious wrongdoings. Even the newspapers followed suit. At that time, people thought that the Party was really being open-minded. It was a snare that many naive people fell for.

The Reaction

Then the Anti-Rightist movement began. "Rightist" opinions generally included the common complaint of peasants that their life was worse than it was before and that the life of workers in the cities was better than that of peasants; and that the policy requiring peasants to sell a high quota of their harvest to the government forced peasants to starve. Other people demanded to cancel the political lessons in schools and universities; to have the freedom to move to other cities or from the countryside to the city; to have the freedom of speech and publication; to criticize wrong-doings in the previous movements; to criticize Chinese interference in the Korean War (meaning the money used in the war should be used instead to improve the life of their own people or for the construction of China); to criticize the Soviet Union for their soldiers who raped Chinese women in 1946 when they occupied the northeast after driving out the Japanese; to criticize one-party rule; to demand equal opportunity in the elections of government leaders (there were some so-called democratic parties in China); and many others.

Mao's Anti-Rightist Movement

However, on June 8, the *People's Daily* ran an editorial, "Why Is this?" on the first page. It mentioned the term "Rightists." On June 12, Mao wrote an article, "Things Are Changing," and circulated it within the Party. On the 14th, the *People's Daily* published another editorial, "The Bourgeois Direction Taken by *Wenhui Daily*." This editorial was rumored to have been written by Mao. It blamed the *Wenhui Daily* and the *Brightness Daily*, two newspapers managed by Party members, for their criticisms of the Party. Thus began the anti-rightist movement.

Mao was said to have commented that the rectification movement was just a trick to "lure snakes out of the hole." Who were the snakes? Mao seemed to mean the rightists. Mao estimated that about five percent of the population in China were "rightists." This was really the kind of subjectivism that was decried (taking one's own view, and using it as the standard of measure), as Mao invented a fixed number of rightists without counting, even when the movement just began. The number should have been calculated only when the results came in. On the 15th of October, the Party issued another document, "Standards by which to Decide on Rightists." There were six rules for determining who were rightists:

1. Anti-socialist system: people who opposed the basic economic policies of the Party and government; negating the achievements of the socialist revolution and construction; insisting on a capitalist viewpoint.

2. Opposing the proletarian dictatorship and democratic centralism, such as resisting the fight against imperialism; disagreeing with the foreign policy of the government; disagreeing with the five movements; opposing the execution of reactionaries; opposing the reform of capitalists and capitalist intellectuals; demanding to replace the laws and cultural education of socialism with those of capitalism.

3. Opposing the leadership of the Communist Party in political life, and in the economy and culture; attacking the leading organizations and leaders of the Communist Party and the government for the purpose of opposing socialism and the Party, slandering the revolutionary activities of the Party.

4. Disrupting the social harmony for the purpose of opposing socialism and the Party, such as instigating people against the Party and the government; instigating friction between industrial workers and peasants; instigating discord among minorities; slandering the socialist camp; fomenting discord among peoples of different socialist countries.

5. Actively organizing and joining cliques against socialism and the Party, such as plotting to overthrow the leadership of the Party anywhere; instigating riots against the Party and government.

6. Aiding, advising, passing information to those who committed the above crimes.

There were 552,877 rightists found in China, out of the entire population of 642,380,000 in 1957. Important rightists included Zhang Bojun, head of the *Brightness Daily* newspaper, Chu Anping, chief editor of that newspaper, Luo Longji, head of the *Wenhui Daily* newspaper, and Pu Xixiu, chief editor of that newspaper. One of the rightists among the capitalists was Wang Kangnian, who insisted that if the government bought people's land and property, they should pay fixed interests for twenty years, not seven years, as the rate was five percent. And this calculation was in line with earlier public declarations.

Actually, all the points raised by the "rightists" were proven correct as history played out. As for the fixed interests, at the end of the seven years, the Party decided to continue paying for another three years. Ten years altogether. Then the Cultural Revolution began and no one mentioned it any more. End of story.

What became of the rightists? Some lost their jobs and were forced to clean bathrooms. Their salaries were duly reduced to the level of a cleaner's. Some were sent to labor reform camps. Hard labor, plus a great famine that took place later, killed many of them by hunger or disease.

All the rightists were given a "rightist cap," as it was called in the newspaper. It was actually an invisible cap, only recorded in their personal files. But the files followed them everywhere they went, so it was like having a cap always on one's head. After 1985, some rightists were restored to full citizenship, but they were still called "uncapped rightists," which meant that though their caps were removed, they were still deemed different from other people.

During the Cultural Revolution those people, capped or uncapped, were criticized and even beaten. In 1977, many false convictions were overturned, including rightist cases, almost twenty years after the Anti-Rightist Movement. By May of 1980, most of the rightist cases were rehabilitated, and they were no longer called "uncapped rightists." About 97% of the rightist cases were judged to have been wrong. But 1978, after twenty years, only a little more than 100,000 of the 552,877 so-called rightists survived. Many victims had died.

On in November 2005, Shi Ruping, a retired professor from

Shandong University, together with some other professors and their families, signed an open letter to the National People's Congress and the State Council demanding that the Party make self-criticism and apologies to the intellectuals who had fallen victim to this political persecution, and give them reasonable and satisfactory compensations. In three months, they garnered 1,500 supporters.

In 2007, on the 50th anniversary of the Anti-Rightist Movement, 61 survivors in Beijing signed an open letter demanding that the Party should openly declare the rehabilitation of the whole Anti-Rightist Movement, not just the individuals. But the Party declined to take any such steps.

Through this movement, Mao and the Party intended to quench all opposing voices and even to stifle dissent in people's minds. Anyone who dared to say anything different from what the Party wanted them to say would get punishment. Mao was said to enjoy reading history books and learning strategies used by ancient military leaders and government officials: stratagems for seizing power, how to defeat political enemies, how to feint and lay military traps, how to appeal to people's beliefs, or ego, diplomatic ploys and salesman's techniques. If he couldn't calculate a harvest, he certainly knew how to calculate to win.

CHAPTER 16. MAO'S GOAL TO OVERTAKE ENGLAND IN 15 YEARS

Barely had the Anti-Rightist Movement been victoriously completed, in November 1957, when Mao put forward another idea: that China must overtake Great Britain in 15 years. Well, he was referring specifically to iron and steel output and certain other major products. Mao headed a delegation to the Moscow to attend the celebration of the 40th anniversary of the Soviet Union's October Revolution. Then he attended conference with representatives of 64 communist parties and worker's parties from all over the world. Mao announced that since the Soviet Union could overtake the US in 15 years, China could overtake Great Britain in 15 years, too.

At that time England's annual steel production was 20 million tons. In 15 years, it might reach 30 million tons. So his aim was to reach 40 million tons in steel production in 15 years. From official estimates of the speed the steel production in China, production would reach 12 million tons in 1959, 30 million tons in 1962, 70 million tons in 1967, and 120 million tons in 1972. This sounds like the same kind of estimates that drove the agricultural policy, but the party leaders thought that their aim could be achieved in 3 or 5 years, no need for 15 years. To find new sources of iron ore, local party secretaries led people in their areas into the mountains, even elementary school pupils and the elderly, people in their 70s and 80s, joined the action. Peasants left their work in the fields and abandoned the harvests to participate in the search for ore deposits. In Henan province, 50% of the grain was left unharvested and rotted in the fields.

By then, the total goal for iron and steel production had been set at 10.7 million tons. An official Party decision to that effect was taken on the 17th of August, 1958. To achieve that goal, they wanted the whole nation to engage in the making of iron and steel. They ordered people to build old-styled open-pit ovens, like in the kitchens of primitive old houses. In all factories other than steel plants, a couple of ovens were set up to make steel on the side. As to where to get the raw materials, they commanded people to take down all the steel doors, iron bars on windows, and steel fences, and to sell all their household goods made of iron and steel, such as tools and kitchen utensils. If people could have cut their food with wooden knives, they would have ordered them to give up their steel knives. This of course reduced production of other necessities and disrupted the supply chain for other goods. As a result of all these efforts, it was declared in December 1958 that the total output of iron and steel was 11,080,000 tons, task victoriously completed. But more than 3 million tons of the steel and 4,160,000 tons of the iron were no good, all garbage. A complete waste of money and materials and labor force. The loss was estimated at about 20 billion yuan in Chinese currency.

Once they had melted the raw material, how did they make the "steel bricks? Here is a description. Whatever scraps of iron or steel were on hand would be thrown in the oven until they melted a little, just enough to stick together. Then the piece was taken out and put on an iron anvil. One man tightly held the half-softened piece on the anvil using long-handled tongs, and two other men hit it in turn with big hammers, while the person holding the piece turned it around, over and over, until it began to take on the shape of a brick. The two men hit the piece by turns, as is often done in hand-forging, as the piece cools quickly and one man can strike while the other is raising his hammer again. As soon as the shape was fixed, the job was deemed finished. This "steel brick" was put aside and they would go to work on the next one. Three men's efforts were tied up working at each oven. That was how the steel bricks were made.

CHAPTER 17. THE MEETING ON MT. LU AND PENG'S LETTER

Background Information

In 1958 when Khrushchev visited Beijing, he derided China's Great Leap Forward as a mania of the petty bourgeoisie. During the period of May–June in 1959, when Khrushchev officially visited Albania, he met Peng Dehuai, who let Khrushchev read a memorandum recording some severe criticisms of the Great Leap Forward and the people's commune. On July 17, Khrushchev made a speech in Poland criticizing the Great Leap Forward and the people's commune. The next day, the newspapers in the Soviet Union and Poland repeated the same criticisms. That set the international background.

Data from the National Statistics Bureau showed that China's total output in 1958 was valued at 130.7 billion yuan, 21.3% more than in 1957; the total industrial value was 108.3 billion yuan, 54.8% more than in 1957; and the total agricultural value was 56.6 billion yuan, 2.4% more than in 1957. The total quantity of grain in 1958 was 200 million tons, 2.54% more than in 1957. Therefore, Mao thought that the policies of the Great Leap Forward and the people's commune were correct. So he refused to accept any criticism, though he admitted that there had been some shortcomings in carrying out the policy, like forcing people to do things against their will, exaggerating, commanding blindly, and allowing cadres to arrogate special rights over people.

The Meeting On Mt. Lu

In July, 1959, the Party held a conference on Mt. Lu, on which Mao owned that there were some demerits in the Great Leap Forward and the people's commune movements, but the Party should yet accelerate the completion of all the tasks of the Great Leap Forward. At first the conference was going peacefully. The representatives toured the mountain in the day and held a dance or had a walk in the evening, besides attending meetings. The purpose of this conference was at first just to let other leaders know these demerits and help to correct them. The conference lasted for nearly a month and all the representatives were happy as it drew to an end. Just then an apple of discord dropped on the table. Peng Dehuai handed in his "Ten Thousand Words Letter" to Mao.

Peng's Ten-Thousand Word Letter

Peng Dehuai was the vice chairman of the central military committee of the CPC, the minister of National Defense, and a vice Premier of the state council. Although the administration was not known for inviting input from anyone, he finally decided that he had quite a lot to say. What did Peng say in his "Ten-Thousand Word Letter"? He just pointed out all the mistakes made so far, with an in-depth analysis. In 1959, he said the Party should slow down the speed of development and not keep on with the Great Leap Forward, which had thrown the economy off balance and created new difficulties. He also sharply pointed out that the exaggerated statistics and the passing of false information to party leaders were just the surface of the problem, the deeper cause being the lack of openness to advice and other opinions (an aspect of democracy) and personality worship, which hit home to Mao's leadership. On July 17, coincidently on the same day as Khrushchev delivered his criticism in Poland, Zhou Xiaozhou, the first party secretary of Hunan province, gave a talk that supported Peng. On July 20, Zhang Wentian, a vice minister in the foreign affairs ministry, supported Peng, too. Mao refused to listen to Peng, and Peng had an argument with Mao. Mao criticized Peng severely, and called Peng and his supporters an "Anti-Party Clique." They were removed from their official positions and put in prison. But the people of China respected them for their courage in speaking out. During the anti-rightist movement over 10,000 party members were criticized and were ill treated. All those cases were redressed in 1962, except Peng. It is thought that Peng's main offense was his failure to protect Mao's eldest son adequately during the Korean War.

A Great Leap Backward into Famine

Largely as a result of the foregoing policies, a serious famine hit China from 1959 to 1961. Some reports suggest that at least 30 million people died from hunger. The high estimation was more than 60 million. As the Communist Party kept such statistics a national secret, no one can be sure. If calculated at 37,558,000 (from official statistics recently revealed), the number is 7.65 million greater than the total number of deaths from starvation in all the history of China, almost equivalent to the casualties in the Second World War, which was between 30–40 million.

The Great Leap Forward and the steel making spree damaged the agricultural sector deeply. In 1960, the grain output fell to 158,000 tons, 26% less than in 1957 before the Great Leap Forward. In Sichuan province, renowned for its plentiful grain production, the output decreased year by year from 1959 to 1961. In 1961, it was even less than in 1949. In that province alone, 10 million people starved to death. Some cadres wrote a letter to the Central Committee of the CPC to tell the truth, but they were decided to be an anti-party clique.

Many in the countryside ate grass and tree bark. The Party denied that there was a famine, but called it a natural catastrophe. It really did not matter what they called it. Later, however, Liu Shaoqi, the chairman of the People's Republic of China, confessed that the calamity was "seven tenths human error and three tenths a natural catastrophe."

Even during the famine years, the Party exported grain in order to earn foreign currency. And in 1959, when people were starving in the streets, 4,157,500 tons of grain were exported to the Soviet Union and other socialist nations in Eastern Europe in exchange for help to develop the military industry. Given the constant menace from the West, as the Cold War raged on, one could say that there was some strategic basis for this deadly trade-off. But on top of that, in April 1960, they gave 10,000 tons of rice to Guinea, and 15,000 tons of wheat to Albania. Was that just a public relations ploy to deny the true state of affairs?

CHAPTER 19. SO-CALLED GREAT CULTURAL REVOLUTION

Background of the Cultural Revolution

During the so-called natural disaster, as millions of people were starved to death, the national economic situation got worse and worse. Therefore, Mao was forced to recede to the background, and Liu Shaoqi stepped into the foreground, helped by Deng Xiaoping, the secretary general of the Central Committee. Mao was not happy to step back from center stage, however, even to evade blame for his own errors. It is possible that this sense of rivalry was a driving factor behind his next invention, the Cultural Revolution.

In January, 1962, at a meeting of 7,000 people, Mao criticized himself for the mistakes he had committed and for having damaged the national economy. That was when Chairman Liu Shaoqi said that it was "seven tenths human error and three tenths a natural catastrophe." But in August of the same year, at the meeting at Beidai River, Mao insisted on his theory of class struggle as the main danger of the present society. Mao thought that there was still the possibility of revisionists taking the upper hand, by which he meant the revival of capitalism. As events developed, one could see that Mao had laid a theoretical time bomb. Liu and Deng Xiaoping failed to read the signals correctly. The Cultural Revolution was certainly a bold scheme. It could have destroyed Mao's position and his reputation forever. Or the whole country might have descended into civil war. In February 1963, the Party Central Committee decided on another political movement, proposed by Mao, indeed, Mao's strategy to retrieve his lost power. Liu Shaoqi, as Chairman of the nation at the time, was of course the nominal leader of the movement. As usual, Liu sent out work teams across the countryside. Liu thought that the target of this movement was the common people, just like the previous movements. The work teams didn't know who the target was at all, and they created havoc.

In December 1964, at a Central Committee meeting, Mao said that it was wrong to aim at the common people. The target (this time) should be the cadres. This was a fairly opaque statement and no one was sure what he intended. So Liu made self-criticism. A trap Mao had set for him to fall into.

Then in January 1965, the Central Committee agreed with Mao that the target of this movement should be those in power within the Party, those who were persisting in going the capitalist road. At that time, no one could guess who that meant. But Mao had a certain goal in mind. Another theoretical trap. According to this theory Mao was the right person going the socialist road, and any other persons who held different opinions were those going on the capitalist road.

All other leaders of the Party tended to act as though Mao could never be wrong theoretically. So this was called the fight between the two roads: the socialist road and the capitalist road. As Mao declared himself to be, and as he was accepted as, the representative of those going the socialist road, Liu was by definition the representative of those going the capitalist road. This was accepted by the others. Liu had already lost. His tragic fate was sealed even before the beginning of the Cultural Revolution, since the others were all confused by Mao's theory and could not find the arguments to properly (and safely) debate him.

However, Mao still let Liu lead this movement, as a Chinese saying goes, "If you want to get, you must give first." Mao was well versed in the stratagems of gaining, keeping, and winning back power once it's lost. Liu, as usual, sent out work teams again. Statistics showed that in the region of Changde town, in Hunan province, 331 persons were criticized, among whom 21 were beaten, 65 bound hand and foot, 3 hung up, and 42 forced to kneel on the ground. In a suburb of Beijing, 40 people committed suicide. Only this time, the target was the lowest cadres in the countryside, not common people anymore, as Mao now planned to use the common people as his chessmen. Pawns can be powerful when they get in a certain position. The Red guards were his chessmen too.

Meantime, Mao traveled all over the country. He talked secretly with some of the top generals to get their support. Among all the generals, two were the most important, Lin Biao, then Minister of Defense, and Xu Shiyou, Commander of the Army for Nanking and Shanghai. With their support, Mao was sure to have his way. However, he had to proceed very carefully.

The Cultural Revolution Begins in the Cultural Field

A public appearance by Mao's wife, Jiang Qing

At that time, most officials in the local governments were supporters of Liu and Deng Xiaoping. This was Mao's problem. But Mao was a master of building consensus first, then he could say anything and use public opinion against his political rivals. So he began with that.

Mao used his wife, Jiang Qing, to help him. Mao had married Jiang Qing while he still was legally married to He Zizhen, sister of Marshal He Long, but she was in the Soviet Union for treatment of a presumed mental disease. Mao and Jiang were in YanAn. This is all described in detail in the later sections of Chapter 3.

Jiang Qing had been an actress before she went to YanAn. She originally lived in Shandong Province. When she took part in some activities against the Japanese occupiers, she had to escape secretly to Shanghai, which was not under occupation. She joined the Left-Wing Drama Union, acting in some revolutionary plays. She was said to have been a better actress on stage than in movies. When she became the wife of Mao, she tried to hide her background since a history as a starlet was not quite the best reputation for a leading lady in real life. In the Cultural

Revolution, most of the actors who had worked with Jiang Qing were put into prison to keep them quiet.

Now, as Jiang Qing had learned to sing Beijing opera, she began looking to make reforms in the area of Beijing opera. This started between 1964 and 1966, after she published an article, "Talk of Revolution in the Beijing Opera." This gave her a bridge which she could cross to take part in political movements later on. When she had married Mao, the Party had banned her from getting involved in politics. But opera reform only involved culture. Maybe that is why this movement was called Cultural Revolution, when it was an actual political revolution in disguise. So far, no one in the Party had any objection. Generally Beijing opera was about ancient stories. The reform was to have new plots relating to modern stories. One title known in China was "Red Lantern." The ballet was reformed, too. Some famous ones were the "Red Detachment of Women" and the "White-Haired Girl."

On November 10, 1965, Mao let Jiang Qing instruct Yao Wenyuan in Shanghai to write an article criticizing the new historical play, "Dismissal of Hairui from Office," published in *Wenhui Daily* on November 30. They published in Shanghai because in Beijing at the time all the officials were Liu's men. The article said that the play was a roundabout way of seeking to redress the case of Peng Dehuai, because Hairui, the main character, was the defense minister in the Ming Dynasty, equivalent to Peng before his dismissal. This play was written by Wu Han, who was a vice mayor of Beijing at the time. He was the first official Mao wanted to get rid of, which would be a breakthrough into Liu's circle.

The so-called February coup d'etat

Mao wanted Yao's article to be published in all the newspapers in Beijing. But Peng Zhen, the mayor of Beijing at the time, thought that such an article was not suitable and so refused to publish it. Besides, as we just saw, the writer of the play, Wu Han, was a vice mayor of Beijing. To support Wu Han, Peng Zhen organized a "five-person Cultural Revolution group" approved by Liu, Deng Xiaoping and Zhou Enlai, the Premier of the State Council, with the intent of limiting the criticism to the cultural sphere, not politics. Peng Zhen had no idea of the full scope of Mao's plan. But Mao would not allow him to stand in his way, so he decided to get rid of Peng as well. As a Chinese saying goes, if you have enough power, you can accuse anyone of a crime and make it stick.

Yao's article connected the play with the dismissal of Peng Dehuai, which smelled of political attack. Mayor Peng thought that theater criticism should stay within the realm of culture and should not connect with political events. On the 13th of February, Mayor Peng summoned a meeting of the five-person group and criticized Yao for connecting his article with a political event. All the attendees supported him in limiting criticism to the scope of culture, except for Kang Sheng, who insisted on the rightness of the article.

The five-person group drafted a report called "February Outline," saying that any discussion in the field of culture must be based on facts, and must respect facts, which meant that connecting the article with the dismissal of Peng Dehuai was not based on facts. On the 8th of February, Mayor Peng, Kang Sheng and Lu Dingyi, went to see Mao and gave him the "February Outline." Mao pointed out that the gist of the play was the "dismissal" and so it did have a connection with the dismissal of Peng Dehuai. Mayor Peng said nothing.

During a 3-day meeting in March, Mao made a speech before the political bureau of the CPC. The gist was that it was very important who had control of the newspapers, magazines and publishing houses; that capitalist authorities in culture must be criticized; that the magazine "Frontline" was controlled by Wu Han, and his supporters were anti-Party and anti-socialist; that a Cultural Revolution must be waged in the areas of literature, history, philosophy, law, and economical theory; that Marxism-Leninism should be more salient in those areas. In conclusion, the February Outline of the five-person group was also criticized. Mayor Peng and his supporters were all sacked and were defined as an anti-Party clique.

It looked as though Mayor Peng and his supporters only had a difference of opinion with Mao. How could they be defined as a clique and accused of plotting a coup d'état? On the 27th of July, 1966, Kang Sheng said in a public meeting in Beijing Normal University that Peng Zhen was planning a coup because he had a battalion of soldiers in every university. The crowds believed him, as he was a party leader. But that was not the truth. The fact was that in February 1966, the central military committee had decided to strengthen the local military forces and maneuvered a regiment into Beijing for training purposes. The soldiers were originally planned to lodge in available rooms at some universities. But as it turned out, the soldiers were lodged elsewhere and didn't sleep at the universities. However, the facts were distorted and Peng Zhen and his supporters were blamed.

Peng Zhen was publicly insulted by Red guards in the Cultural Revolution

How Did The Cultural Revolution Go?

Lin Biao set up the Cult of Personality around Mao

On May 16, 1966, at the meeting of the Party political bureau, a document approved by Mao, was passed around. It was known as the "5/16 Notice" and was deemed the official beginning of the "Proletarian Cultural Revolution." At the same time the "Central Cultural Revolution Group" was organized to replace the "five-person Cultural Revolution group." On the 8th of May, Lin Biao, the Minister of Defense at the time, said that Chairman Mao was a genius, and praised him to the heavens, saying that a sentence from him was worth ten thousand sentences from others. This began the "Personal Worship" or cult of one single personality, the whole nation over.

Anyone said anything disrespectful of Mao, let alone against Mao, was automatically defined as a reactionary and put in prison. Many innocent people were imprisoned during the Cultural Revolution. Fantastic stories were circulated. A person killed a cat and was jailed because the Chinese word for cat is pronounced like Mao. The person killing a cat was deemed to have suggested killing Mao. Someone threw a stone which accidentally hit the picture of Mao hanging on the wall, and he was deemed a reactionary. A person was walking in a park and felt tired. He saw a bench, which was damp from the last night's rain. He put his newspaper on the bench and sat on it. He was arrested because there was a picture of Mao on the newspaper.

Why should Lin Biao set up this cult of personality around Mao? It must have been another of Mao's tactics. It was clear that those supporting Mao were much fewer than those supporting Liu and Deng. Mao, through Lin Biao, set up himself as the object of a "Cult of Personality" like a god being worshiped so that no one dared to oppose him.

Then appeared the slogan of "Four Greats" about Mao: Great Guide, Great Leader, Great Commander, Great Helmsman. Then Lin Biao, or someone else in his name, invented a style of dance called the Loyalty Dance. Generally the dancers held a cardboard sign with the word *loyalty* written on it.

The Red Guards movement

On the 25th of May, Nie, a woman Party leader in Beijing University, together with six men, put up a so-called Big Character poster (Dazibao), criticizing the Party committee of Beijing University and the municipal Party committee of Beijing City. At that time Mao was in Hangzhou. When he was told about it, he praised it, calling it the first Marxist-Leninist Big Character poster in the country. On the same day, an editorial appeared on the *People's Daily*, calling upon ordinary people to join in the movement, to down all authorities.

On the 29th, the first group of Red Guards was organized in the middle school affiliated with Qinghua University. Chaos soon erupted. Students in many middle schools and universities rose to oppose the Party leadership. Quite a few university principals were criticized. Seeing this, Liu sent out work teams in an attempt to control the situation. The work teams designated 10,211 students as rightists and 2,591 teachers the reactionaries.

On the 18th of July, Mao returned to Beijing. On the 24th, Mao held a meeting criticizing Liu and Deng Xiaoping for sending out work teams. Liu confessed that he did not know how to lead the Cultural Revolution movement correctly. Deng said that it was like an old revolutionary meeting with a new problem. That was where Mao set the snare for them.

Naturally, Mao took over the leadership as Liu and Deng did not know what to do. Even if Liu and Deng Xiaoping had not sent out work teams but had done something else, Mao would have found fault with them easily. Either way, the result would be that Liu and Deng were out. This is how politics is played. Now Mao was back in power, and it looked like Liu and Deng were not so much driven out of power but had willingly given up to Mao.

Mao supported the Red Guards. On the 5th of August, Mao wrote a Big Character poster, titled as "Gun Down Headquarters—my big character poster." Mao meant that there was a "capitalist headquarters" somewhere in the Party, implying Liu and Deng Xiaoping, who were already out of power. Then Lin Biao was made the vice chairman of the Party, because he supported Mao in taking power back from Liu and Deng.

At the end of May, the Red Guards started expanding rapidly. On the 13th of June, the Party Central Committee and the State Council issued a notification that the university entrance examination was postponed for half a year. On the 18th, the editorial of the *People's Daily* said that the Cultural Revolution must be thoroughly carried out and the education system must be thoroughly reformed. The entrance examination system must be stopped.

And for more than ten years, no new students were enrolled in the universities, and for many years no classes were held in schools. Thus appeared a gap of education and knowledge between the old generation and the young generation. The young generation lacked education and knowledge. The Chinese culture in general degenerated. Then what were the student-aged people doing? They were all taking part in the Cultural Revolution. Students in universities and middle schools formed Red Guards of their own. Younger children stayed home.

The Red Guards began to travel all over the country to instigate riots. They did not need to buy tickets on trains or buses. That was the Party's decision. All they needed was an armband with the words Red Guards on it. It was easy to make or to get. So other people, who were not students, seized this chance to travel for free all over the nation and went sightseeing.

The whole country fell into chaos. Mao wanted the Red Guards to "destroy four old things," which were old thought, old culture, old tradition, and old customs. But it was not easy to define these. So everywhere the Red Guards went, they burned old books published hundreds of years ago, old paintings—even by famous ancient painters, and broke antique curios and relics. They destroyed old wooden shop signs and replaced them with paper ones written in new names. They even proposed changing the name of Shanghai into "July-First City", but Mao disapproved of that.

Why would the Red Guards want to change Shanghai into July-First City? Because the Party declared that the 1st of July, 1921, was the birthday of the Communist Party of China in Shanghai. But as mentioned in Chapter 1, other data reveals that it was established in August 1920, under the guidance of the Soviet Communist Party. In April that year, the Communist International sent Grigori Voitinsky to China. In May, he found Chen Duxiu, aged 42, and they contacted some revolutionary young men in other cities to build the Communist Party of China.

The Red Guards went to private houses and ransacked and destroyed or took away all the valuable personal belongings. They even beat people to death. Statistics showed that in one month, starting the 18th of August, 1966, in Beijing, the homes of 114,000 families were ransacked, and 85,198 individuals were driven out to go back where they came from. From the 23rd of August to the 8th of September, in Shanghai, 84,222 families were openly robbed. And in Tianjin city, 12,000 families faced the same disaster. Other statistics showed that during August and September, in Beijing alone, the Red Guards got 103,000 taels of gold, equivalent to 5.7 tons, 345,200 taels of silver, 55,000,000 yuan in paper currency, and 613,600 antiques objets d'art. In Shanghai, between the 23rd of August and the 8th of September, besides the large quantity of gold, silver and gems, etc., they got $3,340,000 and other foreign currency worth 3,300,000 Chinese yuan, 2,400,000 yuan in silver coins and 3,700,000,000 yuan of Chinese currency. A Party document confessed that even before that, the Red Guards had already taken 1,180,000 taels of gold, equivalent to 65 tons. That was really the aim of "destroy four old things." Mao and the Party wanted, under this banner, to rob people of their valuables. In broad daylight! This was the final blow to the Chinese "national capitalists." After that, they had nothing worth taking away. They were "safe" now, as poor as a lazy squirrel with nothing in store for winter. The pillaging action affected those who had something worth a little money, but who were not actually capitalists.

The cultural losses were dramatic. In less than one month, more than 6,000 art objects, more than 2,700 volumes of ancient writings, more than 900 ancient scrolls of paintings and calligraphy by famous people, and more than 1,000 stone tablets were destroyed. Irreplaceable, all of them.

As to the death rate during the Red terrorism, official statistics showed that only in Beijing, the capital city, 1,700 people were beaten to death. A massacre took place in Daxing town outside Beijing and during three days, 325 persons were killed by cruel means, including some buried alive. At least 200,000 committed suicide. During the whole period of the Cultural Revolution, there were between 2 million and 7 million deaths, one percent of the whole population in China at that time.

In Shanghai, the Red Guards of the Shanghai Museum went to all the collectors on their list to take all the curios to the museum, they said, for the sake of protecting them, or the Red Guards from Beijing might destroy them. Some collectors even called the museum, asking it to send their Red Guards to their homes and take their curios away. Fortune sometimes means misfortune.

Other things happened in Shanghai during the Red Guards movement. At first, their action was only limited to the streets, destroying old shop signs. When they saw women wearing high-heeled or pointed shoes, they would force them to take them off and they would cut through them with scissors (they always seemed to have something with them). They called it a sign of the capitalist lifestyle, included in the four old things. Once some Red Guards saw a girl wearing jeans. They forced the girl to take them off, and the girl had to run home in her underwear. They laughed.

Then when they heard what their fellow Red Guards were doing in Beijing, they started to attack private houses, too. Mostly they went to big houses, generally those belonging to capitalists. Some stayed in one big house for months, eating the canned food and chocolates that were stored there. Some stole gold and silver articles and diamond rings. Others took away any interesting novels for their own enjoyment. Some of the capitalists were forced to kneel on the ground and were beaten or verbally abused.

Lots of Red Guards went to Canton and tried to break past the border sentinels to rush into Hong Kong. They declared that they wanted to make revolution there, too, but were stopped by the Chinese army. The Red Guards even blamed Kim Il-Sung, leader of North Korea, as going the capitalist road and wanted to go to Korea to arrest him. When Kim Il-Sung heard that, he was so enraged that he ordered the graves of the Chinese People's Volunteers broken up, including the tomb of Mao's son. That was repaired after the Cultural Revolution.

In 1967, in Canton, there raised a wave of activists set on killing those prisoners who had been released from labor reform camps. From the 27th of August to the 1st of September, in six days, 325 of those people and their family members were killed. The oldest was 80 years of age and the youngest was only 38 days.

All the university professors and former middle school teachers were criticized or even beaten. Some professors were forced to crawl around on the college sports grounds. Some were made to stand for long hours in a bowing posture with two arms stretching straight behind, looking like a jet airplane. Just try it; it does not feel like flying. Some were ordered to bow before the picture of Mao for hours, too. At the Shanghai Conservatory of Music, the professors were forced to slap each other's faces in public. Many ancient tortures were revived and new ideas were plentiful.

The power-seizing stage of the Cultural Revolution

Then, the target of the Cultural Revolution changed to the authorities of the local governments, under Mao's instruction. Mao thought that most of them still supported Liu and Deng Xiaoping. Therefore, so-called rebels rose and attacked the local government leaders. They seized power from the leaders and organized "revolutionary committees" to replace the local governments.

Now the Cultural Revolution was in the power-seizing stage, which was Mao's goal from the beginning. It had all begun with a movement targeting lower officials, really a maneuver by Mao to entrap Liu. Then it went on to the stage of openly criticizing a play, in order to get rid of some of Liu's important supporters in the capital, Beijing; then it developed to the Red Guards stage to cause chaos in the country; then, in the chaos, it reached the power-seizing stage. This was the critical stage.

If this part went smoothly and was successful, the last stage would be easy to tide over. The last stage was to put only Mao supporters in the local governments after getting rid of all of Liu's supporters. The Cultural Revolution would thus end as planned.

Many rebellious groups were organized and fought each other for power. Generally, they started with a debate. At that time, people all over the country were learning *The Little Red Book*. Every time people wanted to say something, anything, they had to quote something from *The Little Red Book* first. Even when anyone was writing a self-criticism paper, he had to begin with a quotation from it. So any debate between two groups would consist of the two sides shouting quotes at each other. But no one could persuade the other. It was called a "Quotation Battle" since both sides used Mao's quotations to prove they were right. Debates often devolved into fistfights. But did the quotations from the Little Red Book actually contradict each other, or how could opposing groups both cite from it?

Shanghai became home to the Shanghai Worker Revolutionary Rebel Headquarters. The commander-in-chief of this headquarters was Pan Guoping, a young factory worker. The famous Wang Hongwen was, at the beginning, the vice commander-in-chief, a Party member and a cadre of the lowest rank. On the 3rd of January, 1967, Zhang Chunqiao and Yao Wenyuan came back to Shanghai from Beijing and supported Wang Hongwen in grabbing power from the Shanghai municipal authorities. Pan, being too young, was out, and was only made a member of the revolutionary committee. This event was called the "January Storm," and it touched off a wave of power-seizing actions throughout the whole nation.

The conflict in Huairen Hall in February

Huairen Hall is in Beijing, where the leaders of the Central Committee of the CPC meet. During the "January Storm" in Shanghai, Chen Pixuan, the first secretary of Shanghai municipal party, was afraid the chaos would paralyze the municipal administration and he called Tao Zhu, a member of the central Cultural Revolutionary group on January 3, 1967. Just prior, on December 25, Tao Zhu had tried , to protect the old revolutionary cadres and had a severe quarrel with Jiang Qing, Kang Sheng, and Zhang Chunqiao, who were the ones Mao used to fight Liu and Deng, and their local supporters. After the power shift, it was Zhang Chunqiao who became the head of Shanghai.

When Tao Zhu received the call from Chen Pixuan in Shanghai, he went to see Mao and reported it. Mao looked like he was supporting Tao, while Tao was in his presence. But Tao was soon removed from office. Then, Premier Zhou Enlai, said to be instructed by Mao, drafted a list of old cadres to be protected, including all the first secretaries of provinces. They were escorted to Beijing so that no one could harm them. All except for Chen Pixuan, the first secretary of Shanghai, who was detained by Zhang Chunqiao. This was the fuse that set off the dispute in Huairen Hall.

On February 16, 1967, Premier Zhou summoned a meeting in Huairen Hall. When Tan Zhenlin met Zhang Chunqiao at the gate, Tan asked Zhang why Chen Pixuan was not coming. Zhang said that Chen was detained by the revolutionary crowds in Shanghai. At the meeting, the question of Chen's absence came up again and other senior cadres were also infuriated that the central Cultural Revolutionary group wanted to push aside them aside and take over power into their hands. They were using the so-called revolutionary crowds (who had actually been organized by them) as an excuse to fight the older cadres. Ye Jianying, a leader of the Liberation Army, criticized Jiang Qing and Zhang Chunqiao, and others, for their intention to let the revolutionary crowds attack the army and take command of the army from the senior officials. Ye broke his little finger, he slapped his hand on the table so hard in his anger. If, at the beginning of the Cultural Revolution, the senior cadres failed to realize what Mao and his supporters were really after, by now it was clear that they wanted to push the others aside, or even torture them to death so that they could rule China by themselves.

On February 18, Mao summoned the Central Political Bureau, and taking off his two-faced mask, jumped straight into a tirade criticizing the older cadres, to the delight of Jiang Qing, Wang Hongwen, Zhang Chunqiao, and Yao Wenyuan, the so-called "Gang of Four." This event was literally called "The February Current against the Flow" by the Gang of Four. Then the Central Political Bureau was disbanded and the central Cultural Revolutionary group replaced it, becoming the administrative center of the whole nation.

Just four years later, in 1971, after the event of Lin Biao crashing in an military airplane in Mongolia on the 13th of September, the so-called "Current against the Flow" event was reversed. Mao said that the event had been aimed at Lin Biao. Now that Lin was said to have betrayed the Party and attempted to escape to the Soviet Union, the rest of the event could be redressed.

Armed struggle erupts again

On May 6, 1967, the leftists who supported the Communist Party in Hong Kong began a riot against the Hong Kong government. The riot started with strikes and demonstrations, and it developed to assassinations, bombing and gun fights. By the time it ended in October, 52 people died, including 10 policemen. 1,167 bombs exploded.

Almost everywhere in the country, rebels fought among themselves over the bounty and the privileges that were being redistributed, and they formed different groups and fought one another. Some, supported by the army, got guns. So gun fights broke out. Once, even tanks appeared in the streets. Let us enumerate just a few of the most serious fights.

- February 26–March 5, 1967, in XiNing town of Qinghai province: T55 tanks appeared in the streets and 822 persons died and 1,355 persons were wounded.

- August 2–25, 1967, in Yichun town of Heilongjiang province: 37 government buildings were destroyed and two military camps were gunned down; 1,944 persons died and 1,806 were wounded.

- August–November, in Huaihua town of Hunan province: Rebels occupied some labor-reform farms and factories and fended off an attack by the army; 37,700 persons died or were wounded, including 430 military men.

- June 1967–March, 1968, in Yibin town of Sichuan province: More than 170,000 people joined in the battle, including two army regiments; 43,800 persons died and wounded.

- October 1967–end of May 1969, in Inner Mongolia: 56,200 persons were killed, over 377,000 persons were imprisoned. Over 3,550,000 were involved, one fourth of the population of Inner Mongolia.

- April–July, 1968, in Nanning town of Guuangxi province: 22 battles took place, with 101,000 killed and 74,000 wounded.

- December 1968–February, 1969, in Baoji area of Shaanxi province: Out of 70,000 staff in eight ammunition factories, over 45,400 workers were judged reactionaries and 297 of them were executed, which caused a rebellion. Tanks, armored cars, cannons, and flame-throwers were used. Over 13,300 persons died, including some government leaders.

Later, Mao and the Party strictly forbade this sort of thing and the fighting gradually subsided in August 1968. There was no more fighting after 1969.

But no gun fight happened in Shanghai. The army there was under strict control. The largest event was the fight at the Shanghai Diesel Engine Factory, where 10,000 people were working.

At the beginning of the rebellious period, there were two groups in the factory: one called the East Red group consisting of Party members and cadres, and the other called United Headquarters group consisting of workers and other staff. At first, the United Headquarters group seized power in the factory, since the majority of the workers joined this group, but the East Red group felt that as Party members and cadres they should be in charge. Then fights began between the two groups. When Wang Hongwen became a leader of Shanghai, he supported the East Red group as he was also a Party member and a cadre. But the United Headquarters group refused to give in.

On August 4, 1967, Wang Hongwen sent 10,000 people to attack the United Headquarters group in the factory, and in the front lines were trained firefighters. He did not dare to send army or police force there. The United Headquarters group defended the factory with only 3,000 people. Both sides used mainly axes and steel bars as weapons. The defenders also had some glass bottles with flammable liquids, and they actually shot big nuts using rubber-band slingshots.

Wang Hongwen acted as the commander and 10,000 people surrounded the factory. Finally the attackers used a bulldozer to knock down the gate and rushed in. Every man they caught was beaten up. Thousands of captives with blood all over them walked between two rows of attackers, singing the Internationale, into prison vans. Those who were injured seriously and could not walk were simply thrown into the vans. The women were treated a little better. During the fight, thousands of people were hurt on both sides, although no one died. The next day, the members who had not been in the factory that day were rounded up and arrested one by one.

In all those days of the power transfer, Big Character posters were plastered all over the walls and shop windows, revealing all sorts of information that people generally did not know: stories about the conduct and activities of the central leaders, which had been national secrets before, such as the fact that one leader staying in a special hospital for a minor health problem had raped a young nurse. Such wrong-doings were brushed aside as long as he supported Mao politically. If he was against Mao, this would be treated as one of his crimes. If a common person killed another common person, he would be sentenced to death, life for life. But for a high-ranked cadre, only his rank paid for death of another. If a high-ranked cadre killed a common person, he might just be removed from his office.

Many jobless men also organized rebel groups and went to the Street Committee. They did not seize power from the authorities. They just waited there and if any factory or store or any other place sent in a notice to hire someone, one of them would put in his own name and use the seal to stamp the paper. He took the paper and went to work. At least he got a job this way. The authorities did not dare to prevent these actions, as they were afraid of the mob of jobless people.

Since universities were no longer enrolling students, the high school graduates had to be given jobs. However, there were no vacancies anywhere. Then the government thought of a way to dispose of them. Those students who graduated in 1968 and 1969 were sent out to the countryside to be 're-educated' by the peasants. Sound funny? Given the Communist Party of China's premise that the illiterate peasantry represented backwardness in terms of economic production and backwardness in thinking, how could they re-educate students, who had at least had 12 years of education? Rather, the Party had no money to pay them so they kept those who could not be given city jobs at the lowest subsistence level, while simultaneously re-introducing these relatively sheltered youth to the realities of the hard and primitive life that the majority of the population still had to endure. A way to take them down a notch and prevent the formation of a new "privileged" class with a sense of entitlement.

How did those students fare in the countryside? They had to work and live with peasant families. Life was crude and most found it demeaning. Some students who did not have enough to eat would steal something from the peasants. If they were caught, they got a good beating. Some of them had families with money still saved in banks, and they might receive food parcels from time to time from home. If anyone could give a gift to the leaders, he would get better treatment.

City girls looked much better than village girls. So the sons of village leaders preferred to marry city girls in the village by luring them with personal benefits, or even by force. Some girls did end up marrying into the locally prominent families and found a way to get along.

But a few years afterwards, the Party introduced a policy such that students who had been sent to the countryside could return to the cities where they came from, on certain conditions. They had to still be single, or have certain sicknesses, for instance. Therefore, there were cases of girls who had married locally and then got divorced and went back to their parents. Sometimes two students had married each other. Now, under the new policy, they had to divorce first and apply to return to the city separately; then get married again in the city, or marry someone else.

The one-child policy

At around this same time, life for young couples was made even harder by the introduction of another new policy. Objectively speaking, although this policy may be unjust at the personal level, given the enormous population in China the one-child policy is necessary and correct. In 1950, Na Yinchu, the President of Beijing University and the vice director of the central financial committee, had proposed birth control, but Mao did not listen to him. Unfortunately, he encouraged people to reproduce, just like the Soviets. But after World War II the Soviet Union had lost a sizeable percentage of its population and needed to rebuild, so they encouraged people to have more children. The population in the Soviet Union was only 167 million in the 1950s, while that in China was around 600 million, quite enough mouths to feed. A policy that is correct under certain circumstances may be disastrous in other circumstances. By 1970, the population in China had reached 813 million. So a variety of measures, some of them very harsh, were enacted to roll back the tide.

The policy was successful enough that by 2013, there was some relaxation of the rules. If one parent was already an only child, the family would be allowed to have two children.

Lin Biao's So-Called Betrayal of the Party

Background of the "9/13" event

In March 1970, Mao informed the leadership that China no longer needed such a figure as the National Chairman (as opposed to the Party Chairman, which was Mao's position at the time). Why did he make such a decision? The sense was that since he had stepped down from that position and given it to Liu Shaoqi after bringing China to economic ruin, he could not assume that office again after Liu was driven out, or he would lose face—like a child who had given a toy to someone and then taken it back during a quarrel. People would think that he had not willingly resigned but had been forced to resign as the national chairman. Mao would never do such a thing as he would lose face. A major concern for the Chinese.

Besides, he feared that if anyone else took this position he would surely take away some of Mao's power, just as Liu Shaoqi had done before. He did not need to have such a time bomb by his side. He even suggested revising the constitution to abolish the position.

The National Chairman was deemed the Head of State. A nation might not need one single person to represent it in the world, in theory, but in reality, there has to be a recognized figurehead who receives foreign VIPs or attends international events in the name of the entire nation. A party chairman could not perform the duties of the national chairman. Therefore, Lin Biao, the vice party chairman at the time, and other party leaders, thought that China needed to have a national chairman. Lin took it upon himself to propose keeping the position of the National Chairman. Mao assumed that Lin Biao wanted to take this position himself, though Lin Biao gave assurances that he would never accept this position and even proposed that Mao resume it himself. He did not know why Mao rejected the position.

Different opinions become open at a meeting on Mt. Lu

In late August 1970, the second session of the ninth party conference started on Mt. Lu. Three items were to be discussed for final decisions. First was to revise the constitution. Second was to formulate the national economic plan. Third was to prepare for war, because at that time there was a crisis with the Soviet Union over some disputed territories at the northern frontier.

The most heated debate was over the proposed revision to the constitution to abolish the position of the national chairman. Many representatives supported Lin Biao in asking Mao to accept the role of national chairman, and they also proposed Lin Biao as the vice national chairman. But Mao did not want Lin Biao to have more power as he already had, as the vice party chairman, though Lin Biao showed no desire to usurp Mao's power. He was lawfully decided as Mao's successor.

Lin Biao had quite a few supporters in the People's Liberation Army as he had been commander of the 4th field army in the second civil war. Four of his followers in the army supported him in this meeting and so did his wife. Mao determined that anyone who was in favor of the idea of keeping the position of National Chairman was wrong and should perform self-criticisms. So the four followers and Lin's wife had to criticize themselves, but not to Mao's satisfaction. Mao calculated that Lin was behind all this and so Lin should make self-criticism, too. However, Lin Biao maintained that he had done nothing wrong in proposing that Mao be the National Chairman. He had declared that he would not be the vice national chairman even if Mao was elected the national chairman.

How Mao pushes Lin Biao into a deadly snare

After the meeting, Mao was determined to get rid of Lin Biao just as he had got rid of Liu Shaoqi. He required absolute obedience. So Mao traveled outside Beijing again to make preparations. He went to talk to the army commanders in several major provinces about Lin's supposed intention to become National Chairman, which he characterized as an anti-party act—Mao thought of himself as the representative of the party, and anyone who disagreed with him was against the party. This was the traditional thinking of ancient emperors. Mao also demanded absolute loyalty from the commanders. He warned them to keep these talks secret. But on his own he let the talk leak out so that Lin Biao and his family got wind of it. Mao reckoned that even if Lin was patient enough to wait for Mao's next step without taking any rash action, his wife and son were young and inexperienced, and they must take some drastic measures and would fall into his snare.

The official record said that Lin's son had organized a secret assassination group, called "United Fleet," in case he needed to murder Mao. So when he heard news of what Mao was up to, he plotted to kill Mao using antiaircraft guns against the train Mao rode from Hangzhou to Beijing. He set this up without the knowledge of his father, Lin Biao. But Mao changed his plans in some way, as the Party recorded in the official record, and arrived safely in Beijing. People doubted if there really had been any such plot to murder Mao. However, the official report to the public said that when their plot failed, Lin's wife and the son sought to escape to Canton, to set up another central government against Mao's in Beijing. On the 13th of September, 1971, Lin's wife dragged Lin, who was sick in bed, out of the house and pushed him into a car to drive to an airport. When they boarded a military plane with the son and some followers, they were told that the plane did not have enough fuel to fly to Canton, and so they decided to fly to Russia instead, as Lin had been in Russia previously for medical treatment.

Then the Party told the whole nation that an accident happened and that Lin, his wife and his son died in the plane in a crash in the Mongolian Republic. How could a leader's plane just crash? The explanation was not so satisfactory. Then a rumor circulated that the plane was downed by a missile from within the area of Inner Mongolian, just as the plane was crossing the border into the Mongolian Republic. The commander of the army stationed there was General You Taizhong. In communist China, rumors were often the closest one could get to real news. Facts were circulated in the form of rumors, or the Party might declare certain facts to be rumors when they could not deny the information some other way.

Many years later, Zhang Ning, Lin's son's girlfriend, wrote a book narrating the event. She was with the Lin family at the time. According to her, readers might conclude that Lin's death was a trap set by Mao and Zhou Enlai, the premier. As stated earlier, Mao had let out a rumor that he wanted to have Lin arrested or even killed. This successfully inspired Lin's wife and son to try to escape. Lin's chief bodyguard Li got into the car first so that Lin's family members would naturally follow. But when the Lin family got in the car, he jumped out. He shot himself in his left arm so that he would be sent to a clinic for treatment. If he had accompanied the Lin family, he would have died in the crash, too. He must have known what was coming. When Lin's car sped away, the soldiers guarding the place could easily have stopped it, but no one took any action. The Lin family got to the military airport and climbed on the plane that was reserved especially for their use. A few minutes after the plane rose into the air, it seemed that the plane wanted to re-land, but all lights in the airport were out and the runway was dark. How could that happen? It seemed that all this was arranged beforehand. They had to fly north. The Party added an excuse to explain why Lin was trying to fly to Russia, taking the shortest route. As the plane crossed the border, it entered the territory of the Mongolian Republic.

Although the Chinese people doubted the details, they did not care that Lin died. He had supported Mao, or the Cultural Revolution would not have happened. There is a Chinese saying that when there are no more rabbits, the hunting dogs will be cooked. Lin was a typical example. It was said that Mao wanted to wipe out all the old cadres who had been part of the Long March and YanAn in order to make way for the Gang of Four: his wife Jiang Qing, Wang Hongwen, the vice chairman of the party at that time, Zhang Chunqiao and Yao Wenyuan. Later, Mao wanted to wipe out Zhou Enlai, too. His intention was as plain as the nose on his face.

The Movement to Criticize Lin Biao and Criticize Confucius

On the 18th of January, 1974, Mao called for another movement, in short, "criticize Lin and criticize Confucius." What did Confucius have to do with Lin Biao? They lived thousands of years apart. It was said that after Lin's death, Lin's rooms were searched and some quotations from Confucius were found written on paper stuck on the walls. And Lin had said that Mao was like the first emperor of the Qin Dynasty, the tyrant, who had buried alive hundreds of scholars and burned books he did not like. This began to resemble Mao's anti-rightists movement against intellectuals. That was why Lin and Confucius were combined for criticisms.

Then at Mao's instruction, "criticize Zhou" was added. The slogan became "criticize Lin, criticize Confucius and criticize Zhou [Premier Zhou Enlai]." After getting rid of Liu, and then of Lin, now Mao wanted to get rid of Zhou Enlai to clear way for the Gang of Four to take over the national power. But as all the old cadres supported Zhou, and as Mao knew that Zhou Enlai was wise enough not to fall into any trap, Mao had to let this movement slip by without any results.

The April 5 Movement in 1976 on TianAnMen Square

Background of this movement

After Liu Shaoqi and Deng Xiaoping were out of their leading positions at the beginning of the great Cultural Revolution, they had different destinies waiting for them. Liu was dying of diabetes and was lying in bed in a hospital with tubes in his nose and throat. In October 1969, Lin Biao ordered Liu to be moved to a prison in Kaifeng city of Henan province. He was put on a stretcher without clothes on, only covered with a blanket. He was flown to the city in a military plane. He caught a cold and then pneumonia. He was thus thrown into a special cell in the prison, and was found dead on the 13th of November, when a nurse came to check on him. So his body was sent to a crematorium and burned to ashes. On the paperwork his name was listed as Liu Weihuang, not Liu Shaoqi. His job title was given as "vagabond," not chairman of the People's Republic of China. His conviction was overturned in February of 1980.

As to Deng Xiaoping, when Liu was carried to jail, he was sent to labor in a factory repairing agricultural tractors in Xinjian town in Jiangxi province. Luckily for Deng, the leader of the factory had been one of Deng's subordinates in the war period and so took good care of him. Deng just did some light work. In February, 1973, Deng Xiaoping returned to Beijing. When Premier Zhou was found to be suffering from cancer, Deng Xiaoping was appointed to take charge of state affairs.

On the 19th of May, 1975, in a routine checkup, Zhou Enlai was found to have cancer of the bladder. The doctors in charge reported it to the Central Committee of the CPC and got their instructions: first, no more examinations; second, no operation; third, don't tell Zhou or his wife. This decision was made by the Gang of Four. They wanted Zhou to die as soon as possible, and on the 8th of January, 1976, he obliged. In accordance with Premier Zhou Enlai's will, his ashes were not put in an urn and buried in a specific place but were spread on the land of China. One very unpleasant tradition in ancient China was that anyone in power could dig up the body of his enemy and flog the body to vent his fury. Zhou Enlai did not want to keep his ashes in any special place, lest his tomb be desecrated and his urn be insulted some day, when the Gang of Four came to power.

The April 5 event

On the 4th of April, 1976, the tomb-sweeping day for the dead, people in Beijing gathered on TianAnMen Square in memory of Zhou Enlai and criticized the Gang of Four (without mentioning their names). The crowds were estimated at 2 million. So that night, police were sent to clear the square of the funeral wreaths and slogans and also began to arrest people, a process that went on till dawn of the 5th day. There was a three-storeyed house in the southeast corner of the square used as a command center. Angry crowds burned some cars and surrounded the house, demanding to talk with someone in charge, but they were refused. So the crowds set fire to the house, but those inside escaped and no one was hurt.

That night, over 10,000 militiamen, five battalions of soldiers and 3,000 policemen rushed to the square to disperse the throngs. As the militiamen, soldiers and policemen only carried wooden sticks, no guns, no one was killed. The Gang of Four thought that Deng Xiaoping was behind this, as the crowds on the square had shouted their support of him, and so on the 7th of April, Deng was out of office again and put in confinement. Then Hua Guofeng was appointed the Premier and the first vice chairman of the Central Committee of the CPC.

This movement was defined as a "reactionary" event. In November of 1978, the case was redressed and all those who had been arrested and put in prison were set free.

The Arrest of the Gang of Four and the End of the Cultural Revolution

The downfall of the Gang of Four with the death of Mao

After the death of Lin Biao, Mao's health deteriorated. In 1972, he had a serious shock: he was suffering from cataracts and was partially blind. In 1975, an operation restored some of his sight. On the 9th of September, 1976, he died at the age of 83, with no clear diagnosis mentioned. His title at the time was Chairman of the Central Committee of the CPC, the chairman of the central military committee of the CPC, and the honorary chairman of the Chinese People's Political Consultative Conference. So he was only the head of the Communist Party, not the head of the nation of China. But as he was the chairman of the military committee of the CPC, he was the most powerful man in the country, because in China, the military forces were controlled by the Communist Party, not by the government, or the nation. That was why he had given up the position of Chairman of the Republic, but not the position of the military committee of the CPC. Before his death, he appointed Hua Guofeng as his successor, as he clearly knew that none of the Gang of Four, not even his wife Jiang Qing, had the abilities necessary to administrate such a huge country as China. If he had appointed his wife as his successor, the old cadres would surely oppose his decision. But if he appointed one of the old cadres, the Gang of Four and their followers would object just as well. By contrast Hua Guofeng, though he was also not fully capable of taking on such responsibilities, was acceptable to both sides. In any political move, a politician should aim for balance among all sides, and then he can stay safely in the center.

The Chinese people knew that the Gang of Four was supported by Mao only. Now when Mao was out of the picture, the Gang of Four would not stay long in power. And now Hua Guofeng faced a choice: which side should he favor, the Gang of Four or the old cadres. A wise man could see which side to choose. Hua was a wise man and stood with the old cadres.

The Cultural Revolution ends with the arrest of the Gang of Four

Just after the death of Mao, Jiang Qing, as Mao's wife, demanded Zhang Yufeng, Mao's personal secretary, give her the key to Mao's safe. Zhang refused, saying that everything belonging to Mao belonged to the Party. The key had to be given to the chairman of the party, Hua Guofeng. Jiang had to leave without the key. What was so important in Mao's safe? It contained the top secret documents of the party and the state, and some letters that revealed certain incriminating personal secrets with which various high-ranking cadres could be blackmailed, besides Mao's bank information and check book. Whoever controlled those documents and letters could control certain persons, or even the state power. Zhang reported this to Hua Guofeng, and Hua came to understand the importance of Mao's safe. He sent Wang Dongxing, Commander of the central security bureau for the safety of the party and national leaders, to take care of it.

On the 21st of September, Jiang Qing and Zhang Chunqiao recommended Li Xing as the commander of the central security regiment. They wanted Li to report to them all the information of the security regiment and addresses of all the members of the political bureau, how their residences were guarded, etc. Li promised to give them all the information they wanted, but at the same time, he reported to Wang Dongxing and then to Hua Guofeng.

Both sensed the danger of a coup from the Gang of Four. Before Mao's death, Mao's nephew, Mao Yuanxin, had been appointed the liaison officer between Mao and the Central Political Bureau. Naturally Mao Yuanxin worked under Jiang Qing, Mao's wife. At dawn on the 4th of October, 1976, Li Xing heard Mao Yuanxin informing the Gang of Four at breakfast that he had maneuvered two divisions from Shenyang military zone to station themselves just one day's distance from Beijing. Li immediately reported to Hua—if summoned, these forces could reach the capital in one day.

Hua decided that he must take action at once. So he went to see Li Xiannian and Ye Jianying, two old cadres in charge of the army. They decided to call the Gang of Four to a meeting and arrest them then and there. Meanwhile, they notified the commander of the Shenyang military zone to order the two divisions to return to their original camps.

Wang Dongxing was entrusted with apprehending them. Zhang Chunqiao came first and was caught in the dark corridor to the meeting room without any trouble. Then Wang Hongwen was apprehended and pushed into the room, when he suddenly struggled out of the grasp of the security guards and dashed at Ye Jianying, with the intention of getting a grip on Ye's neck; but he was stopped and handcuffed only one meter from Ye. Yao Wenyuan did not offer any resistance when arrested. Jiang Qing, quick-tempered as always, threw a heavy porcelain vase at the guards but was subdued after a brief struggle.

In the morning of the 25th of January, 1981, the Gang of Four were judged at court. Jiang and Zhang Chunqiao got the death sentence, but suspended for two years; this generally meant the prisoner would not be executed in the end but the sentence would be commuted to life in prison. Zhang Chunqiao said nothing at court, in a display of contempt. After two years, Zhang's verdict was accordingly changed to a life sentence, in January 1983, and in March 1993 his sentence was changed to 18 years, but in January 1997, he was released for medical treatment. He died of cancer on the 21st of April, 2005, at the age of 88. At court, Jiang Qing protested volubly and even gave some sort of a speech, though apparently she would have benefited from the assistance of a professional speech writer. In January 1983, her sentence was also commuted to life in prison. On May 4, 1984, she was released for treatment of throat cancer. But on May 14, 1991, she hanged herself in the bathroom using several handkerchiefs tied together. She died at the age of 77. Wang Hongwen was sentenced for life and in 1986, he was moved to a hospital in Beijing where he died of liver disease on August 3, 1992, at the age of 58. Yao Wenyuan was sentenced for 20 years and was duly released on the 6th of October, 1996. He died of diabetes on the 23rd of December, 2005.

The Chinese people watched the whole process on television like they were watching a drama. A political spectacle for people to enjoy, nothing more. It was just a fight within the Communist Party, like dogs fighting for a bone—political power. Whoever won the game had nothing to do with the common people. The winner became the king and the loser became the prisoner, in accordance with a Chinese saying.

Thus ended the great Cultural Revolution and thus began a new era for China. Good or bad for the Chinese people? There are always winners and losers.